The Swing Era
1940-1941

EDITOR: George G. Daniels

Staff for THE SWING ERA 1940-1941   EDITOR: Philip W. Payne   ADMINISTRATIVE EDITOR: Jeanne
LeMonnier ART DIRECTOR: John R. Martinez STAFF WRITERS: David Johnson, Joan S. Reiter, Michèle Wood
RESEARCHERS: Betty Ajemian, Lea Guyer, Helen Harman, Suad A. McCoy, Florence McNeil, Joan Nierenberg,
Karl F. Reuling, Barbara Richey, Eleanor Schwartz LAYOUT: Leonard S. Levine COPYREADER: Rachel Tucker-
man CONSULTANTS: Dan Sibley (graphics), Joseph Kastner, George T. Simon (editorial)

MANAGING DIRECTOR: Francis M. Scott III

GENERAL MANAGER: Peter L. Hoyt PROMOTION MANAGER: William C. Kiefer
SALES MANAGER: Edmund Schooler BUSINESS MANAGER: Terrance M. Fiore
PRODUCTION MANAGER: John D. Hevner INTERNATIONAL OPERATIONS MANAGER: Charles C. Colt, Jr.
EUROPEAN MANAGER: Robert H. Smith ASIA MANAGER: Beto Yamanouchi

THE SWING ERA is produced in the United States by TIME-LIFE RECORDS in cooperation with CAPITOL RECORDS,
INC. David D. Cavanaugh, Executive Producer, Bill Miller, Associate Producer. Editions outside the United States and
Canada are produced in cooperation with Electric & Musical Industries, Limited, London, England, or its affiliated companies.

ON THE COVER: Stanley Catron and Kaye Popp, both 17 and both then appearing in the Broadway musical *Something for the Boys*,
demonstrate for Gjon Mili's camera one of the steps of the Lindy Hop. The picture first appeared in the Aug. 23, 1943 issue of LIFE.

The Swing Era

How It Was To Be Young Then

The Men Who Made the Music:
  Glenn Miller
  Harry James

The Music in This Volume

Discography

1940-1941

TIME-LIFE RECORDS

NEW YORK

How It Was To Be Young Then

Growing up in the '30s and '40s was like putting together one of the jigsaw puzzles that lay half-finished on wobbly-legged card tables in a million American living rooms. On rainy Sunday afternoons we worked to complete Rembrandt's *Night Watch* in all its 1,000-piece glory, or an Olde English Hunting Scene. Collectively we were also assembling, with bits of our lives, an even grander super puzzle with a bewildering variety of pieces: bread lines, banana splits, rationing coupons; DC-3s, trolley cars, Model A Fords; Mickey Mouse, Albert Einstein, Lili Marlene; Count Basie, Eddy Duchin, Glenn Miller; Scarlett O'Hara, Dale Carnegie, Li'l Abner; jukeboxes, nylons, bubble gum, K-rations, gardenias, bombsights, saddle shoes; love and hate, life and death.

Who were we, the young of the Swing Era, the joiners of this giant jigsaw? We had names like Allen Ginsberg, John F. Kennedy, Jesse Owens, Bill Mauldin, Frank Sinatra, Oona O'Neill, Mary McCarthy, Eartha Kitt, Gloria Vanderbilt, Jackie Robinson, Norman Mailer. Malcolm Little would be better known someday as Malcolm X. Thomas Lanier Williams would become Tennessee. Whizzer White would move up to "Mr. Justice White." Grace Kelly would be addressed as "Your Highness," Richard Nixon as "Mr. President."

Most of us, though, would be famous only to our friends. We were named John Dickinson, JoAnn Phenis, Roberta Carnes, Joyce Furgie, Herbert Spohn, Robert Zang, Benjamin Gim, Ginny Hoyler, Ralph Goodpasture—and the person I remember best from the Swing Era, Joan Swallow. I can't find her in the mirror, but she turns up in old photographs.

The first piece in the puzzle was Home. Home was a

two-story frame house on the outskirts of a small city in eastern Indiana. Inside it dwelt the statistically average American family: father, mother, 2.3 children. The 2 were my older brothers, the demigods of Home; the .3 was me.

My home was the center of the universe, and it was gratifying to learn, as I grew up, that others thought so too. Our state called itself the Crossroads of America and for 50 years had contained the Population Center of the U.S.A., a movable title that has since drifted west to Illinois. I finally grasped the idea by imagining the country as a large, irregular plate laden with 130,000,000 beans held aloft by Charles Atlas with his forefinger just under Sullivan County on the banks of the Wabash.

Muncie, where my cousin Charline lived, was much closer. It turned out to be a hotbed of something called "contemporary American culture." People named Lynd (he was a New Albany boy) had gone there to study the phenomenon and written a book about Muncie, giving it an entirely different name, *Middletown*.

"Heartland" was another thing people called us in books, though no Hoosier would have used the word—too highfalutin. The "Nation's Breadbasket," in which we were sometimes included, got closer to the gut facts. "Corn Belt" was best of all.

This Blessed State, this Happy Median was at the very navel of the universe because we lived in the greatest nation that had ever existed, the freest, most powerful and best—America. The Depression had brought hard times but, now that Roosevelt was in, most people felt that happy days were here again. Or soon would be. We children stood in our classrooms and sang with all our hearts:

> America, America,
> God shed his grace on thee,
> And crown thy good with brotherhood
> From sea to shining sea.

Like America itself in the '30s, our house was half in the country and half in the city. My father started life as a farm boy but found his livelihood in towns. In 1910 my newlywed parents set up housekeeping in the tiny community of Economy, Ind., where my father was cashier at the bank. He built his own home, eight years later, just beyond the city limits of Richmond, the county seat. He could drive to work, two miles away in the center of town, in ten minutes, but on his three acres, remote from sidewalks and traffic lights, he created a miniature farm.

Behind the house was his garden with rows of leaf lettuce, spring radishes, green onions, butter beans, carrots, string beans, peas, beets, cabbages, onions and potatoes—and the two most succulent of Indiana crops, tomatoes and sweet corn. Fruit trees made May beautiful with clouds of pink and white blossoms: Maiden Blush and Transparent apples, red cherries (good for tart, juicy pies if you could get them before the birds did); two plum trees in the chicken yard where our White Wyandottes pecked happily at windfalls; even a grudging peach tree.

We had berry bushes, clumps of asparagus and rhubarb, and an arbor of Concord grapes. In the pig lot, far enough back to be out of nose-reach, half a dozen Poland Chinas rooted and grunted and slurped watery milk from their trough. In the calf lot we sometimes fattened a young Hereford or Black Angus steer. I never ventured into the cow pasture, most remote of the acres, until I was big enough to meet Buttercup, the Jersey, eye to eye. Beyond the pasture lay The Woods where the world seemed to come to its northern end.

In the back yard was a modish sunken pool, edged with flagstones, where water lilies bloomed and big goldfish swam. From its center rose a birdbath in which dusty sparrows liked to sport; honeybees drank from its lip, stinging me when I tried to pick them up for a closer look. On a swing, hung between two stout poles, I lunged fiercely at the sky, hovered, and fell back again.

We could watch the seasons pass across our lawn. Spring came with furry gray nubs on the pussy-willow bush, followed by violets, tulips and narcissus. On Decoration Day we cut peonies and blue flags, which we never called "iris," for the family graves. On warm early-summer nights, as fireflies began to flicker and June bugs crashed against window screens, we rocked in the front-porch swing and inhaled the scent of mock orange and honeysuckle. In the terrible heat waves of summer we dragged ourselves from room to room seeking the breath of air that would bring sleep. The heat waves ended in still more terrible storms—they don't make lightning and thunder like that any more.

The sound of katydids in August meant frost in six

Not all of the young in this Swing Era sampler were famous then. Movie stars Jackie Cooper, Freddie Bartholomew and Mickey Rooney *(below)* romp at a pool.

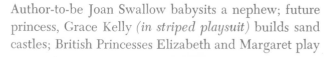

Author-to-be Joan Swallow babysits a nephew; future princess, Grace Kelly *(in striped playsuit)* builds sand castles; British Princesses Elizabeth and Margaret play

weeks. We were too busy stuffing ourselves with sliced tomatoes and corn-on-the-cob, fresh from the garden, to pay attention; but when we heard the first cricket in the house we knew the maple leaves would soon turn red and yellow and that all too soon the early twilights would lie blue upon the snow.

Winter was an indoor time. Our house seemed to be standard: living room, dining room, kitchen; three bedrooms and a bathroom upstairs; front and back porches; attached garage; cellar. Like the cow, the hand-stoked hot-air furnace had to be tended twice daily. We had no television, no dishwasher and no air-conditioning in our house, not even insulation. No refrigerator. We had an icebox, filled regularly by an iceman. In summer his truck drew kids like flies to sugar, and Mr. Shores, though he grumbled, never refused us a piece of ice to suck.

Bedrooms were different then. People were born in them. *I* had been born in the east bedroom, with Dr. Fouts attending, late on a Saturday afternoon, my father somewhere in the vicinity and able to report at once, to my brothers reading the funny papers downstairs, that they had a sister. It's a pretty picture until you remember that, with all her family within earshot, my mother had to be brave, like it or not.

Mother kept us from missing the "conveniences." She loved her family, she loved keeping house. Her love was expressed in the snowy shirts my father wore to the office, just enough starch in their collars and cuffs; the smooth, cool sheets on our beds, smelling faintly of the outdoors; the hot butterscotch-pecan rolls on the dining-room table; the pitcher of fresh lemonade on hot evenings; the feather-light angel food cakes on our birthdays. She had been a working girl once, clerking in George Mosey's store in Greens Fork, Ind. Both her sisters worked; Aunt Sue was a widow, Aunt Mae a grass widow. But it never occurred to my mother that there was any role in life preferable to hers.

This little world of childhood, My House, sounds idyllic, remote. It wasn't, though; it never is. I could hear the great world beyond at night, when things were quiet: it came blowing down through The Woods, the sound of "The Spirit of St. Louis" hooting at the crossings. The sound of trains as one lay in bed, still awake, is an unforgettable part of those years. Johnny Mercer listened to them too and wrote, in *Blues in the Night*: "Hear the train a-callin'/Whooooo-eeeee/Hear that lonesome whistle blowin'."

The great world beyond was even closer than the Pennsylvania Railroad. At the foot of the front yard lay U.S. 40, the National Road. A statue in the city park, the

with the royal Corgis. At 16, Gloria Vanderbilt sits on steamer trunk with her aunt, winner of a famous custody battle over her niece. At Whittier College, Richard Nixon plays a pipe-smoking innkeeper; and at Harvard, Norman Mailer plays football. At 17, Norma Jean Baker strikes a pre-Marilyn Monroe pose.

Madonna of the Trail, reminded us that the pioneers had come this way. And it was still the Way West.

Let me live in a house by the side of the road/Where the race of men go by, Sam Walter Foss had written, seemingly with us in mind. U.S. 40 never palled. The single most important event of my summer mornings at age 6 was the passing of "the interurban." The conductor and I always waved to each other. The interurban was an electric railway car that ran from Indianapolis to Columbus, Ohio; it was like the streetcars we rode in town, but sleeker, higher, faster and more perilous. Its track paralleled the road and crossed countless driveways. Even before the National Safety Council began issuing its lugubrious holiday forecasts, we had had the sound and sight of several bloody disasters on the National Road West etched into our nervous systems.

Some of the car traffic turned in at our driveway: the Watkins Man, a kind of traveling drugstore; the Fuller Brush Man. I sat at the other end of the living room and listened raptly to their spiels. How cleverly they revealed hidden, ground-in dirt in the carpet! How magically they removed it! The Magazine Salesman ("I'm working my way through college") came too. The Encyclopedia Salesman painted a grim picture of incipient mental malnutrition, only to be staved off by buying the six-volume *The New Home Interest Library.*

Eva Clevenger, next door, had an even more arresting parade of visitors. Like many people in the '30s who had spare bedrooms, she hung a sign out front: "Tourist Home." It brought in a dollar or two on a good night. One group of travelers remains indelibly in my mind (and in Eva's). They extended their stay a day or two, getting very cozy with the family and relaxing everyone's guard. Then one afternoon when the coast was clear, they whipped everything light and portable into their cardboard suitcases and were gone. "Even the doily under the lamp," moaned Eva, "even the toilet paper." The general conclusion was—Gypsies!

Pedestrians of the Depression

> Beyond the blue horizon
> Waits a beautiful day. . . .

Increasingly, a special kind of pedestrian turned off 40 and came up our drive. This was the hobo whom the Depression had made rootless and had set wandering across America. Tramps knocked at our back door for something to eat. When nothing better was available, my mother handed through the screen door slices of bread spread with butter and sugar. We watched through the curtains as the tramp returned to National Road and started west again, walking backward and jerking his thumb for a ride.

We were among the lucky who did not go hungry during those years. Plenty did. There were families like Malcolm Little's, outside Lansing, with nothing to eat some days but a big pot of boiled dandelion greens; on better days it might be corn-meal mush, or mush in the morning and cornbread at night.

The times were hard on teen-agers who could not afford schooling or get jobs. In 1935 nearly one out of four youths who had reached employable age since October 1929 was neither employed nor in school full time. But the New Deal, dashing down the dike from one leak to the next, did not overlook the young. The Civilian Conservation Corps was among the most popular of all New Deal measures (even diehard Republicans liked it), and a pet project of President Roosevelt, who saw to it that the first contingent reached camp only six weeks after his inauguration in 1933. The CCC, all volunteers, were mostly young men from the cities between the ages of 17 and 23, unemployed and single. A Corpsman received base pay of $30 a month, $22.50 of which went to his family if it was on relief. At its peak in 1935, the Corps employed more than half a million young men in 2,600 camps, and in its nine-year life it enrolled a grand total of 2.5 million. These civilian conservationists did indeed conserve a lot of their country, planting a billion trees, half of all the trees ever planted in the U.S., restocking streams with fish, fighting forest fires, halting erosion. The National Youth Administration, another New Deal measure, helped more than two million young people to stay in high school or college by paying them to improve their own communities and schools.

The poet John Ciardi, a Boston boy saving money for college, earned $14 a week in 1933 working nights as a shipping clerk. That was about standard for a recent high school graduate. A man with a college degree might get as much as $20. My oldest brother, Charles, a 1932 graduate of Earlham College, landed his first decent job late in 1933 as an outside man for the Personal Finance Co. in Cincinnati, calling on slow accounts and checking on new loan applications. A car was essential.

"Dad gave me his 1928 Model A Ford Sedan and I took off," Charles wrote to me in a reminiscent letter. "Pay was $90 a month plus $45 monthly allowance for your car. We received a rebate on phone calls made to the office, so the trick was to find a free phone whenever possible but to turn it in as paid. At the end of the month you were able to collect three or four dollars, a great help in those days.

"In September 1934 Ruth and I decided to get married. As it was nearing the end of the month, I was broke. Thanks to her father, Ruth had some money so she bought the ring ($6) and paid for the license. We rented a flat—two rooms and bath, utilities included, for $22 a month. We had no icebox and kept our perishables in a window box. Ruth used the landlady's washer for laundry.

"Life was good. We had a tough time lasting out the month, though. We learned you could take a milk bottle back for five cents and put four cents with it and get a loaf of bread. We went home to Richmond every two weeks, sometimes oftener, more to get two or three

On a summer evening, the corner drugstore is a great place for improving social graces through conversation.

A swing band coming direct from some glamorous locale, like Glen Island Casino, lightens the load of homework.

meals plus take-home goodies than because we were homesick.

"Stephen came to us in October 1935. Ruth went home to her mother's before he was born. In those days Reid Hospital charged $25 for delivery and a week's stay. Dr. Kreuger also charged $25 but that included care before, during and after."

In 1935 Charles and Ruth moved back to Richmond, a $17-a-week job and a $15-a-month apartment. "On Saturday night we would have Opal and Frank Slattery over and we would play bridge. Roasted peanuts from Tracey's were three pounds for a quarter and we would have a quart of beer; Ruth would make a 10-cent spice cake to go with our coffee later."

My other brother, Bud, was not quite 14 when the Crash came and the Great Depression got under way. I asked him how teen-agers fended for themselves in those days.

"I got a yard to mow once in a while through the summers of the early '30s," Bud wrote back, "and this was good for 25 to 50 cents. I sold packets of flower and garden seeds and made a little. Another fellow and I sold balloons along Highway 40 a couple of summers— mostly on Sundays when the traffic was out. We blew them up by mouth and fastened them to a stick or on a string. I can remember tying two or three on car-radiator ornaments and watching the fellow drive on with his girl, and hoping they wouldn't start to break until they got a ways down the road at least."

Factories were firing men then rather than hiring, but Bud earned enough at odd jobs for some social amenities.

"Things were cheap then. If you could not afford cigarettes at a dime a pack, you bought a sack of Bull Durham and rolled your own.

"On dates, if you were lucky, you walked to somebody's house and later down to the corner Coke place, where a fountain Coke with lots of ice was five cents. So you might only be out ten cents for the evening.

"Movies in 1932 and 1933 were only 20 cents or 25 cents. For a dance date the admission was one to two dollars per couple. You could afford this once in a while and generally borrow your Dad's car or double with someone who could get one."

Everyone needed a laugh in the '30s, and fortunately almost every American home had a magic laughing box called radio. It was an age of great comedians—Amos 'n' Andy, Jack Benny, Fred Allen, George Burns and Gracie Allen, Fibber McGee and Molly. I was a kid who had had my mouth washed out with soap (an experience, I find, that lasts a lifetime) for being too sassy, so I reveled in the sass of Charlie McCarthy.

I found radio's Little Orphan Annie a bore, but I choked down Wheaties in order to send away for Jack Armstrong's Shooting-Disc-Gun, and the Whistle Ring that enabled you to send code messages to beleaguered friends. For a while I was a devotee of Dorothy Hart and her Sunbrite Junior Nurses' Corps, but trying to

9

round up empty Sunbrite Cleanser cans for my nurse's badge became too onerous. Even skulking down alleys in east Richmond, en route home from my piano lesson, I could seldom find a trash pit that contained one.

Richmond's favorite radio stars were the home-towners who had made good. Richmond housewives faithfully followed the network soap opera "Betty and Bob" because Will Reller's beautiful daughter Elizabeth played Betty. Everybody got a kick out of knowing that Elizabeth had spent two years at the Royal Academy in London getting rid of her Midwest accent, then had had to recover it in a flash when she broke into radio in Chicago, doing Junis Facial Cream commercials for Amos 'n' Andy.

If your family had no radio, there was still plenty of fun to be had, most of it mercifully free from the super-vision of adults.

Alfred Kazin, the writer and critic, grew up on Chester Street in the Brownsville section of Brooklyn, and he recalls, in *A Walker in the City*, that "We worked every inch of [our block], from the cellars and the back yards to the sickening space between the roofs. Any wall, any stoop, any curving metal edge on a billboard sign made a place against which to knock a ball; any bottom rung of a fire escape ladder, a goal in basketball; any sewer cover, a base; any crack in the pavement, a 'net' for the tense sharp tennis that we played by beating a soft ball back and forth with our hands between the squares."

Boys' games in the old days—before adult super-vision set in—were naturally rich in violence and ag-gression. A good thing, too, in the opinion of Bil Gilbert, writing in *Sports Illustrated*. When he and his contem-poraries played king-of-the-mountain, capture-the-flag, pioneer-and-Indians ("really nothing but loosely orga-nized rumbles . . . the idea is to knock down or beat up other players") they worked off their hostilities in ways "untainted with subterfuge or twinges of guilt." Mum-blety-peg developed nerves of steel, as players took turns flipping a knife to make it stick into the ground.

An Indiana boy also had to find plenty of time to practice basketball, sometimes using for a hoop a peach basket with its bottom knocked out nailed up over the garage door. Boxing held a special attraction for black kids, because, as Malcolm X says in his autobiography, when Joe Louis became world champion, "Every Negro boy old enough to walk wanted to be the next Brown Bomber." Malcolm was no exception.

Many of us spent a lot of time doing nothing. I liked to climb up on the pighouse roof and just sit there, studying the shapes of clouds and mulling over interest-ing questions such as why Amelia Earhart looked ex-actly like Charles Lindbergh. And it was delightful to lie in the grass and observe the movements of ants, or climb up in the trees and watch the leaves tremble in the wind. The intensity with which our senses re-sponded to the physical world is, in retrospect, among the greatest joys of childhood. Eartha Kitt describes it in her own story, *Thursday's Child*, remembering the early years in rural South Carolina when she was sepa-rated from her mother and living among strangers.

"I spent many hours in the pine woods gathering pine cones. I would lie in a sunny spot and think of the Heavenly Father. I would watch the few planes that passed overhead, wondering where they were going, where they had come from, what made them fly, and if there was a little man inside to make them run . . . I lived in my thoughts and when my thoughts and seren-ity were broken, I felt hate unless Nature did it. . . . When it rained, I loved the rain—to run in it, to soak my feet in it, to wet my bushy brown hair in it, though I could never get it dry again. I belonged to Nature and Nature belonged to me."

William Zinsser, growing up on Long Island's North Shore, also spent a lot of time watching things, like boats on Long Island Sound. He recalls, in *Five Boyhoods*, that his favorites were the Fall River Line steamers *Priscilla* and *Commonwealth*.

"One of them passed every night at six on her voyage to sonorous Fall River, surely an enchanted place if it could beckon these noble vessels with such unswerving regularity. Sometimes I could hear the music of their bands, and if I waited 20 minutes the waves would lap up on our beach, all power spent but a link nevertheless with the traffic of the seven seas."

The game of Monopoly which came upon us in the early '30s united us in juvenile lust for money and power, and also united adults and children. When the generations felt like fraternizing, we also shared the pleasure of Sunday drives. Seeing how many different license plates you could spot was fun; so was watching for white horses. The real treat, though, was finding a new Burma-Shave sign like:

THE BEARDED LADY		FELLOW SPEEDERS
TRIED A JAR		LET'S REHEARSE
SHE'S NOW	or	NOW ALL TOGETHER
A FAMOUS		GOOD MORNING
MOVIE STAR.		NURSE.

Thus we rolled over the great plain of childhood—which had, nevertheless, its unexpected elevations and sudden drops. There were terrible ordeals sometimes, like Bill Mauldin's when he had to be a bridesmaid (there was a shortage of girls) in a Tom Thumb wed-ding at his grade school in Mountain Park, N. Mex. There were thrills, too, when for instance you were the little girl that got to hand a bouquet to Mrs. Franklin D. Roosevelt. There were scares. Billy Zinsser was terrified of kidnappers. "A shadow of fear fell over my life when the Lindbergh case broke. The papers reported the story in more detail than I cared to know, yet I pored over every word and photograph, hoping to learn something that would be useful when my time came. The worst picture was one of the ladder leading to the baby's open window, for *my* window was much nearer the ground, where any fool could reach it." And there were triumphs. Malcolm Little was a newcomer to town when he entered junior high school in Mason, Mich., yet "in the second semester of the seventh grade, I was elected class president. It surprised me even more than other people. But I can see now why the class might have done it. My grades were among the highest in the school. I was unique in my class, like a pink poodle. And I was proud; I'm not going to say I wasn't."

Early in 1931 the *Literary Digest* published a survey of vocational preferences among boys and girls between the ages of 8 and 18. The grown-up boys wanted to be aviators, architects, lawyers or electrical engineers, in that order. The little boys chose cowboys, aviators,

soldiers, army officers, again in order. Girls of 18 were hoping to become typists, stenographers or housewives. Girls of 8 and 9, however, wanted to get into the movies.

Little Frances Gumm was one of the first to make it, aided by her family's theatrical connections, and emerged from her chrysalis as Judy Garland. Julia Jean Mildred Frances Turner, born in Idaho in 1920, was actually discovered in a drugstore by the editor and publisher of a Hollywood trade paper who asked her, "How would you like to be in pictures?" She had a walk-on role in her first movie, wearing a sweater and a skirt, and became Lana Turner, America's sweater girl.

Norma Jean Baker didn't have to make her way to Los Angeles: she was born there in 1926 and was steeped throughout childhood in movie lore. She was working in a defense plant when a photographer spot-

This four-door 1938 Ford V-8 Deluxe Convertible was popular with the young set long after vanishing from the ads.

ted her. His picture story led to work as a model and eventually to fame and fortune for Norma Jean as Marilyn Monroe.

A special group

"Teen-ager." According to the *Dictionary of American Slang*, "The U.S. is the only country having a word for members of this age group, and is the only country considering this age group as a separate entity whose influence, fads and fashions are worthy of discussion apart from the adult world. Before 1935 U.S. teen-agers considered themselves as, and were considered, young adults and not a special group."

I like this fact but am not sure what to make of it. Perhaps it simply means that we were the vanguard, the first of the Visigoths to appear on the frontiers of the Empire and test its defenses.

What is adolescence, anyway? A period of preparation—often exhilarating, often harrowing—with a forward motion taking you inexorably to that point when you will commit yourself: to a specific vocation, to a chosen partner (or to a life without a partner), to a life-style. No wonder we got scared at times.

Teen-ager is only a word, and yet it meant something: it meant *us*. Words had once been no more than objects, mere shuttlecocks that you tossed back and forth in spelling bees. Now it was clear they could have important, personal meanings. "Character," a word beloved by our parents and teachers, had dominated our childhood; you were supposed to have a good one and develop it. It often had disagreeable associations, like

being smartly rapped about the shins with an apple-tree switch if you told a lie. Whatever desire we had had for "character" temporarily yielded to the more insistent lure of "glamour," "personality" and their by-product, "popularity."

Glamour was fairly comprehensible. Brenda Frazier was its epitome. Brenda was beautiful, rich, famous, and socially prominent. O.K., I concluded, glamour was out.

Personality seemed to be more within my reach. It was a mysterious but not unattainable commodity. You bought it and applied it externally, like Tangee lipstick, or Ipana-for-the-smile-of-beauty. You also developed it on your own, by enlarging your biceps à la Charles Atlas, or your bust with exercises carefully detailed in *Good Housekeeping*, or by suppressing your own crude self and impersonating someone more winning. ("I declare, Betty Ann, blue is certainly your color." "Dave, is it true you have carried the ball more yards than anybody else?") Movies offered valuable pointers. Bette Davis, obviously, was loaded with personality. For at least three hours after a Bette Davis movie, I devastated my circle (they pretended not to notice) with my surly swagger and deadpan hauteur. Books, too, could help—like *How To Win Friends and Influence People*. Civic Hall was packed when Dale Carnegie came to deliver his message in person.

In preparation for high school, the arena for the main events of the teen years, even those of us who felt unable to achieve glamour or personality struggled to acquire "social graces," the prevailing euphemism for not picking your nose in public and getting across a dance floor without falling.

We tend to assume that everybody goes and always has gone to high school. In 1930 only 51 percent of eligible teen-agers were enrolled, versus 94.1 percent in 1968. The age at which youths might legally leave

school once varied greatly from state to state; and, indeed, when society was less industrialized, secondary education was often not necessary.

In a community like Richmond, Ind., during the '30s and '40s, some left school as soon as they could, on their 16th birthday. A Quaker family or two would send the young away to a Friends' boarding school, and occasionally wealthy parents sent a girl to Tudor Hall at Indianapolis. But by and large, the 1,000-odd youngsters attending Richmond's senior high school represented every class and condition in town: both colors and all economic strata, ethnic groups and religious affiliations. It was a good feeling, spending those three years with all one's contemporaries. High school was, of all the social institutions I have been part of, the closest thing to a microcosm.

A community's single high school must be all things to all men. Of the 330 graduating seniors in the class of 1942, 40 percent were in the "Academic" course following a traditional college preparatory curriculum. Twenty-nine percent were oriented toward careers in commerce or office work. Nearly one-fifth of the class, 19 percent, were enrolled in "Boys' General" or "Girls' General"; this meant, for example, that the girls studied "household chemistry" instead of the academic variety. The remaining 12 percent were future machinists, welders, draftsmen, woodworkers and printers.

More impressive than the variety of curricula is the range of extracurricular activities. The high school faculty, some one of whom served as adviser to each of the special-interest groups, were a race of heroes. Besides the usual sports there were tennis and golf teams, a tumbling club, a Ping-Pong group, two fencing clubs with a total of 60 members, and "sports study" clubs for spectators. The print-minded worked on the school newspaper, the yearbook, or the literary annual. The Dramatic Society put on plays. A boys' swing band,

an all-girl orchestra, and a boys' glee club supplemented the regular band, orchestra and choir. There were aviation clubs, a photography club and four different art groups, not to mention a garden club, a conservation club (all boys) and "Rural Girl in Defense," some 20 charmers who posed for their yearbook picture in blue denims, leaning on hoes and pitchforks. The war contributed to swollen enrollments in two Red Cross clubs. A heightened awareness of far places, which would burgeon during the postwar years, already was visible in two "Around the World" clubs, a "World Affairs" club, and a club devoted to "Foreign Correspondence" (overseas pen pals). There was a cinema club, a science club, an archery club, an electricity club, and a club called "Latest in Literature." Debaters and future statesmen joined "Junior Forum." There were even Carver-DuBois and Phyllis Wheatley clubs which were not so much forerunners of today's black nationalism as refuges: the colored six percent of our class still had to sit, like their parents, at the backs of city buses and movie houses.

'Be Central! That's who!'

Central!	Big Apple?
Be Gentle!	Susie Q?
Be Brutal!	Red Devils!
Be Central!	That's who!

Basketball had been for decades the grand passion of Midwesterners. Galesburg, Ill. is said to remember Carl Sandburg as a scrappy right guard who captained the 1900 Lombard team and had a promising future until he turned to poetry. Basketball fever built up slowly, starting in late autumn and mounting steadily through the season to the last regular game in February. Then came the annual statewide tournament, a four-week elimination contest which progressed from Sec-

Still beautifying the U.S. are some of the one billion trees planted during the nine-year life of the CCC.

tionals to Regionals to Semifinals to Finals. For every team in the state, no matter how small, this could be Glory Road, and David-and-Goliath dramas played themselves out to the hysterical cries of fans. Defeated Goliaths took it gracefully: there was always next year.

The hard core of zealots in every basketball town are the high school students and their parents (and their sisters and their cousins and their aunts). But even families temporarily lacking a high schooler followed the team's fortunes on the radio, and the state

tourney was as impossible to resist as a World Series. A Richmond High School girl's role in this group frenzy could be highly satisfying: she joined the booster club and worked hard for a place in Block R, the school's official cheering squad which occupied a special section, the best seats in the house, at each home game. "Working with the pep and precision of the Rockettes," says the 1942 yearbook, "these girls cheer the team and entertain the fans with clever stunts, songs and yells for each game, using red and white cards, balloons, tassels and miniature megaphones. The outstanding stunt this year was the displaying of a replica of the American flag, while they were singing 'God Bless America' "!

Secret societies were banned from our high school, but a group of eight girls from Block R, obeying the gaggle or bevy instinct, found themselves gathering most Friday nights after games to eat monster banana splits at Wheeler's. Soon we adopted a name, the R.O.D.s. We bought identical red hats and sewed onto them the white letters "R.O.D." Our sole corporate purpose was to enjoy ourselves and to stand out in the crowd, and we had no "secrets" except the meaning of R.O.D. itself. It is still a secret, because most of the R.O.D.s have forgotten what those letters stood for.

There were at least four formal dances a year, delicious occasions when you got dressed to the nines. How the feminine eye can still mist over as we glimpse, down the halls of memory, the dresses we wore to our senior dances. For a December dance, the simple but elegant red velveteen, and over it a floor-length white wool cape trimmed with scrolls of gold leather. The spring prom gown: drifts of pale-blue net trimmed in blue marabou, the off-shoulder neckline edged in self-ruching, worn with slender choker and bracelet of rhinestones. The commencement dance dress, for a warm night in June at an outdoor pavilion: the long, full, tiered skirt of waffle piqué in a glorious floral abstract print of apple green, lilac, black and white, colors that Renoir might dream on an April night; the bodice of white eyelet piqué, its neckline edged with beading threaded with black velvet ribbon. "Thank you," we said to our admirers, "I made it myself."

The arrival of the florist's delivery van on Saturday afternoon with the gardenia sent by your date meant the dance was practically beginning. No one publicly exhibited herself in hair curlers then, so somebody else went to the door while you stayed upstairs performing the various rituals which could sometimes be accomplished, taking time out for supper, in as little as four hours. By the time your date had arrived and made five minutes of halting conversation with your parents, you were ready to descend to, you hoped, looks of amazement and awe.

The school gym, with lights dimmed and draperies drawn to conceal the stands, was a stage set awaiting its actors. A specially imported swing band enveloped us in languorous, romantic music like *Moonlight Serenade* which urged us to dance cheek to cheek. (A girl who wore her gardenia on the right side was either inexperienced or not overly fond of her date.) A fine, jumping number like *In the Mood* made us want to jive and bounce.

Special excitement and suspense attended the year's biggest dances, when two lucky maidens were chosen to reign over the festivities: the Queen of Hearts in February, the Prom Queen in spring.

Some insist we were a very innocent generation. Others deny it vigorously. In my high school, thanks to the combined vigilance of faculty and family, we were, on the whole, innocent. We seldom said anything stronger than "darn," and when really provoked we followed the example of Joe Palooka's pal Jerry and exclaimed "!*#¿*!*!" There was very little smoking (actually I can't remember any), almost no liquor, certainly no drugs, and very little promiscuity. Only an occasional high school girl earned a yearbook accolade like "A delightful companion at any hour." Heterosexual affairs existed but were not flaunted. Other types of sexual activity were kept so private that most of us were completely unaware of aberrant behavior.

If you do not find yourself and your peers in the ambiance described above, you may do better glancing through the findings of Dr. Alfred Kinsey, the revolution-maker for whom our generation provided so much raw material: Ninety-five percent of males were sexually active by 15. Maximum activity occurred at 16 or 17. Eighty-five percent of married men had had premarital sex and 50 percent were unfaithful. Sixty-four percent of married women had engaged in premarital sex of one kind or another and 50 percent had had intercourse before marriage. Twenty-six percent had been unfaithful. One-sixth of women interviewed had achieved sexual climax prior to adolescence, one-fourth by the age of 15. Maximum activity occurred between 35 and 40.

If you were old enough to get laid (has anyone ever explained why males use this verb in the passive voice?), you were about ready for another badge of adulthood: your driver's license, which gave you occasional access to the family car. For daytime éclat you tried to get a jalopy. Few were as lucky as my classmate John Dickinson who drove a vintage automobile that had belonged to his grandfather some 25 years earlier, and was too beautiful to mar with decorations. And finally you achieved that other carte d'identité, your Social Security number, setting your foot on the path that would lead, 30 years later, to horrors like the "Chemical Bank Master Charge Statement Simplifier," a 3½-by-9-inch document that arrives each month with the statement and is the computer world's equivalent of *A Skeleton Key to Finnegans Wake*.

Charles A. Lindbergh (*above*) and Amelia Earhart were alike in looks and in their daring flying exploits.

When I rewind my personal soundtrack to its beginning and cut out the radio, the first pop music I hear comes from a Victrola at my grandmother's house. A quavery voice sings:

> Good morning, Mary Sunshine,
> And how are you today?

The tape spins on. After long patches of hiss and sputter, a piano sounds a limpid, silver-blue chord of four notes. Try it: in the left hand, thumb on A below middle C, little finger on the B below; in the right hand, thumb on the D next to middle C, middle finger on G-flat. Play them together and you have the opening of Duke Ellington's *Sophisticated Lady*. As an introduction to the great popular music of our time, you can hardly do better than this subtle, cool, moody, elegant, perfect work. Much of the quality of the music is built right into it. Even a child of 11, if she gets the notes right and maintains an even tempo, can almost do it justice.

The sheet music of *Sophisticated Lady* materialized on our piano one day after it became apparent to the family that there was a lasting affinity between me and the instrument. The name Duke Ellington meant nothing, but if he had written a song my brother Bud liked, I would learn it. Soon a second piece appeared, another beauty which I added to my repertory. This time it came from my father: Hoagy Carmichael's *Stardust*.

Both the Duke and Hoagy had a connection with Richmond that I was unaware of then. One of our local factories, the Starr Piano Company, opened in 1916 a recording division called Gennett, pronounced like the name "Jeanette." Gennett no longer exists, but its fame will endure as long as there is an early-jazz buff. Recently I was dumbfounded to see, reverently displayed in an ambitious Italian publication called *Storia della Musica*, a picture of a warehouse-like building with the caption "Exterior of the Gennett record factory at Richmond, Ind." It stood beside the Whitewater River, smack against the C. & O. railroad siding. Musicians making recordings for Gennett had to suspend operations while trains chugged noisily by.

History sometimes gets made in just such unlikely places. The great Bix Beiderbecke made his first record, *Fidgety Feet*, in that building, with a group called the Wolverines. The year was 1924. The first Hoagy Carmichael number ever recorded, *Riverboat Shuffle*, was a Gennett product, and so was his first recording of *Stardust* (originally an instrumental). Hoagy was also at Gennett the day that his friend Bix with Tommy Dorsey and a few others improvised *Davenport Blues*, named in honor of Bix's Iowa home town. Six of the earliest Duke Ellington records were issued by Gennett, sides like *If You Can't Hold That Man* and *You've Got Those Wanna Go Back Again Blues*.

Meanwhile a surprising amount of good if not historic music was being made in other parts of Richmond, as it was in similar towns the country over. Paul Kring's 17-piece band was good enough to play in New York, for six months during 1925, in the Broderick & Felsen Revue at the Colony Theatre, 53rd and Broadway. Back home in Richmond, dances at the Elks Club, the

Small-town youngsters make a party of a June afternoon haywagon ride through fields of ripening grain.

Soft drinks, doughnuts and some records are enough to turn a living room into a ballroom on a Friday evening.

country clubs, the Leland Hotel ballroom, the pavilion in Athletic Park, the annual Hallowe'en masked ball at the Coliseum—all used live dance music, provided by groups like Paul Kring's.

As the Big Bands era arrived, Richmond's coterie of musicians found additional work as fill-in men for touring bands. Every big-name band arrived in town needing at least one instrumentalist, frequently more, to fill in for absent members. These pickup sidemen had to be able to read instantly the music for the third or fourth trumpet or saxophone part. Naturally the substitute musicians made their own informal ratings of the touring groups. Lowest place went to the band leaders who brought only a hard core—the rhythm section plus the lead men of other sections—but allowed the public to believe it was seeing and hearing the real thing. Sitting in with Duke Ellington's band, noted for its skilled and highly individualistic sidemen, was a stiff challenge for local musicians. A black man who played bass had been lucky enough to fill in with Ellington once; the other Richmond musicians considered this the peak achievement of their group.

A Richmond friend my age got some glimpses into this world because his father was a former professional jazz musician with many friends in the business. Some mornings, especially during the mid-'30s, he would find three or four transient musicians sleeping in the house, trying to save money from their skimpy pay by staying over with a friend. He recalls: "One night Paul Whiteman's Orchestra had played a job in Richmond and gone on elsewhere. About midnight I was awakened by someone pounding on our front door. It was the middle of winter and there was snow on the ground. A fellow was standing there with no coat on, and there was a taxi stopped in the street, with the driver standing outside holding an overcoat. 'Is this the Coate residence?' the fellow asked, and I said, 'Yes.' He said, 'My name is Paul Wingate. I'm a friend of your father's, I play tenor sax—I work with Paul Whiteman—and I need a place to stay.' I said, 'Well, fine, I'm sure that's O.K.' He waved to the taxi driver, who got back in the car and drove off, and then he explained that he'd been hanging out in a bar after the job, and had spent all his money and missed the band bus. So he'd hocked his overcoat with the taxi driver, if the taxi driver would bring him to our house.

"Well, he was obviously far out of it by then, so I had him lie down on the couch, which was all he cared to do, and go to sleep. I went back to bed. In the morning, my brother Jim and I got up early and went downstairs to see this fellow Paul Wingate. He was just awakening. 'Are you really with Paul Whiteman?' we asked, because that was the peak of big-time stuff to us. He said he sure was. We got my father's tenor saxophone and asked him if he would play.

"So about 9 o'clock in the morning he started producing sounds we'd never heard on a tenor saxophone —big, very full sounds— and from the upstairs bedroom my father called out, 'Is Paul Wingate down there?' He could tell from the tone; nobody else could produce a tone that sounded like Wingate. He wound up staying with us two or three days, which was how long it took for my mother to figure out how to borrow enough money . . . to get Wingate's overcoat back from the taxi driver and to buy him a bus ticket to wherever the Whiteman band had gone."

The Big Bands had snuck up on us gradually. Back in the days when the family had an Atwater Kent radio

The high school gym is transformed into a crepe-paper paradise as these celebrants of the Junior Prom, self-consciously

—the kind with a storage battery that you took to the filling station to recharge—my brother Charles used to lie on the floor with his ear at the radio speaker, the better to hear Earl ("Fatha") Hines broadcasting from the Grand Terrace cafe on the south side of Chicago. On Saturday nights he listened to a radio program that featured "society" bands across the continent, starting at the Royal York Hotel in Toronto, then on to the College Inn of the Hotel Sherman in Chicago, next the Brown Palace Hotel in Denver, and winding up at the Mark Hopkins in San Francisco. Such musical tours, multiplied thousands of times in American homes, helped to create an enormous public of swing fans. Swing was probably even more pervasive than rock today, because, though it had its stuffy opponents, it found acceptance among some people at every level: sweet swing appealed to the older folks, and kooky swing—like the inspired corn of Spike Jones, for example, which is even now an excellent baby-sitter—attracted little kids.

solemn in tulle or in dark suits and white buck shoes, begin the grand march.

Jalopies are transports of joy, and a boy's ultimate in automobiling is a casual, manly spin (*below*) with a pretty girl beside him. But first come hours of labor (*above, left*) to make the thing run and the loving application of graffiti to conform to youthful convention.

By the late '30s we were trying to do-it-yourself. Lots of us had learned to play instruments, either at school or with bands sponsored by the American Legion or the Elks. What more natural than to play "swing" in our spare time? In 1939 I was part of a seven-man group (the oldest was a tenth-grader) that bought a few published arrangements and practiced them together. We had a clarinet, a sax, a trumpet, a trombone, a violin, drums and piano. Our repertory included numbers like *Deep in a Dream, My Reverie, Ferdinand, Two Sleepy People*, and, when we wanted to shake the rafters, *Alexander's Ragtime Band*. Our sole appearance, as I recall, was at the opening of Jones & Farmers, a farm-implement store. Roberta Carnes and I, the two girls in the group, stepped to the microphone at one point and duetted *Umbrella Man*. A seasoned farmer can take just about anything, and our audience bore up manfully. Mr. Jones paid us $5 for the afternoon's work. We spent it all on new music.

It was Juke Box *Friday* Night for Richmond teenagers, many of whom went to the weekly dance at the YMCA. The jukebox there was programmed to play all evening—no nickels required—and kids frequently went without dates, boys and girls matching up after they got there. But dates were welcome too. In those days a jukebox was the best sound system we had a chance to hear. A few of us owned portable record players, with speakers that were feeble at best. I had only a turntable, but somehow the sound picked up by the needle came out through our radio speaker across the living room, through an "open" frequency. Whether at the Y or at record parties in our homes, we danced to the same great Miller and Dorsey and Goodman and Shaw numbers that kids were listening to all over the country: *String of Pearls, Begin the Beguine, Frenesi, And the Angels Sing, Green Eyes, Snootie Little Cutie*. Many of these were the same tunes we heard on Saturday night when we listened to *Your Hit Parade*, a review of the Top Ten of the week.

(At the well-lit YMCA we danced in surroundings that were all our parents could wish for. They thought our capers there were a good outlet for surplus teen-age energy. But many Americans felt there was something immoral about swing and jitterbugging. A 1938 article in the New York *Times* quoted a psychologist who thought swing was "dangerously hypnotic" because it was "cunningly devised to a faster tempo . . . than the human pulse." Young people exposed to it would probably "break down conventions." As late as 1942, jitterbugging was forbidden at all Duke University dances—although, the yearbook noted, "certain students independently refuse to obey rules of dignity and grace.")

'A Big Band in person'

The great thing was to see a Big Band in person. The pinnacle of teen-age status in New York was to be present at the Paramount when the Goodman band rose up from the depths swinging *Let's Dance* to the joyous screams of its fans. During the band's weekday appearances, classrooms around New York could be half-empty. The Brothers on the faculty of Manhattan College used to head straight for the Paramount whenever Benny played there, and Evelyn Bennett remembers how the Manhattan College boys waiting in line would suddenly have to duck and run at the sight of a too-familiar figure. It was a Saturday, however, when Helen Harman had a particularly memorable Paramount date with her Lincoln School classmate Alex. Alex lived in the Hotel Pierre, Helen in the Columbia University area. So Alex's mother's chauffeur drove Alex uptown to collect Helen, then returned downtown to deposit the young pair at 43rd and Broadway. They were early enough to get seats in the first row. They saw the stage show featuring their idols, the Goodman band. Then they saw the movie. They saw the stage show again. They slept through the movie. They saw the stage show a third time. It was about here that Goodman took pity on the first row and sent them some hot dogs and Cokes.

Sometimes the Big Bands came to Richmond, but more often they appeared in larger communities nearby. The dance pavilion at Lakeside Park in Dayton was a favorite resort of Richmond couples. My brothers remember Herbie Kaye there, with his vocalist Dorothy Lamour, and Phil Harris with his luscious gal singer Leah Ray. In my day there were groups like Jimmy Dorsey with dimpled Helen O'Connell, and Alvino Rey who did weird and fascinating (and prophetic!) things with his electric guitar, the first amplified instrument I had ever heard. My greatest thrill came one night when the Stan Kenton band was playing at Lakeside. At the end of a set, urged on by my date, I approached the great man and asked him to show me the opening bars of *Artistry in Rhythm* on the piano. He did so, most graciously. I can play them to this day. If I ever meet Stan Kenton again, I'll ask him for the next eight.

You could also hear good live swing on college campuses. The Blue Devils of Duke were led by an undergraduate named Les Brown; the University of North Carolina had first a Hal Kemp and then a Kay Kyser student band. Even a smaller school like Miami University in Ohio had the Campus Owls, an excellent swing band that not only played for big Miami occasions like the Pan-Hellenic Dance but had a wider reputation that kept them working off-campus the year round. Some summers the Owls even went to sea on ocean liners. Playing in dance bands was one way students in the '30s could finance their college educations.

About one in every eight Americans between the ages of 18 and 22 was attending college in 1930, a ratio that persisted throughout the decade with only a slight dip in the bad years of 1932-34. Your choice of school was often pre-determined, either because Dad had enrolled you in Yale '34 at birth, or because State U. was the

Ubiquitous swing: a young drummer practices a para-diddle in the parlor; a couple sorts a stack of the latest records for an evening's entertainment; and youngsters in a Chicago settlement house mob Benny Goodman to get a closer look at that magical clarinet.

one place where you could get a scholarship. By and large, you had to decide between prestige and the opposite sex if you went to college in the East. In other parts of the country we had discovered coeducation a hundred years earlier.

Once the school had been chosen, girls as usual agonized over the problem of what to wear and consulted *Mademoiselle,* whose college issue each August was the freshman's Bible. In the early '30s coeds wore mid-calf dresses and silk stockings, but by 1940 the daily uniform was skirt, sweater, saddle shoes and bobby sox. The number and variety of a girl's sweaters constituted a status symbol, with extra points for angora and cashmere. Dirndl skirts were popular for warm weather and were easy to make yourself. Bandanas, sometimes called babushkas, covered the head. Brief respites from the saddle shoe were provided by sabots, huaraches, and espadrilles, and the loafer achieved lasting popularity. For formal dances the long ballgown reigned throughout the period; it was hard to tell which was sexier, the low-cut Ina Ray Hutton style of the '30s, or the strapless of the '40s. A curiosity of women's dress was the adoption of increasingly masculine attire. This was partly feminist: slacks said you were a free soul, like Marlene Dietrich; mannish suits proclaimed that you could handle a demanding job. Blue jeans, which girls took up en masse in the '40s, were loved for their comfort and practicality. Wearing your boyfriend's sports jacket was another form of "being pinned." And during the war, the regulation Marine shirt which you wore lounging around the dorm stood for the absent one himself.

It was all so simple for men. What did they need on campus except slacks, some shirts and sweaters (including an Argyle knit by the girl friend), a sports jacket or two, a tan raincoat (preferably dirty), and maybe some white bucks?

'The rites of rushing'

The statelier clothes in your wardrobe were chosen with an eye to the rites of rushing. Fraternities and sororities were like the Blue Grotto of Capri: so highly touted, so hard to get into, that having come all that distance and—with enormous bother—finally squirmed in, you *had* to believe it was worth it. Every college had its cliques: Mary McCarthy's *The Group* were eight Vassar girls of the class of '33 who had the South Tower of Main Hall all to themselves and were considered high-hat. But Greek-letter members sometimes found themselves in even more confining molds: inherited traditions which dictated "correct" behavior, a cultivated rivalry with other campus groups, a conscious policy of exclusion. The irony of relinquishing your freedom of social intercourse while simultaneously trying to "broaden your horizons" did not occur to many of us until later. Meanwhile it was great to display on your sweater the pin that said you were one of the elite.

To demonstrate conclusively their worthiness to join the elect, pledges submitted to hazing. On some campuses it was mild: making a symbolic pledge paddle (no one actually struck you with it) and doing a few chores for the members. Elsewhere it seemed like puberty rites in New Guinea: girls in a Pasadena sorority had to swallow "worms," grovel in the dirt, smoke cigars, massage each other's hair with molasses and raw egg, and—crowning indignity—vow never to steal a sorority sister's man. The solemn rituals of formal initiation could be impressive unless someone got the giggles—say, one of the trio of upperclassmen who had to sing, on cue, the three notes of the Mystic Chord.

Fraternities made life more interesting with parties, dances and picnics, but somehow I feel most nostalgia for their serenades. On my campus it was the Betas who did this best, singing *How'd You Like To Be a Beta Sweetheart?* at the freshman dorms in the fall, returning at Christmastime with carols and Beta ballads. And there were lovely, special serenades under the window of each girl that a brother pinned.

Looking through college yearbooks of that era, you get the impression that campus life might have come unstuck without the three great binders of bridge, beer and cigarettes. Somerset Maugham is supposed to have said that with three partners for bridge you can get

through any crisis in life. But even two will do, and in a pinch you need only one victim for that anemic game miscalled "honeymoon" bridge.

One particularly harsh winter in the '30s, three adults in my family spent the bleak January evenings playing three-handed bridge, and they allowed me to sort and lay out the dummy. The disease I contracted then became dormant with the approach of spring and mercifully did not resurface until college, when a virulent epidemic broke out. Men and women were felled indiscriminately; whole fraternities and sororities were laid low.

If you had bid six hearts, doubled and redoubled, and it turned out that your partner didn't have the king after all, naturally you lit up a Lucky. Or a Camel or a Chesterfield or an Old Gold. In the depths of World War II, when Lucky Strike Green *and* Lucky Strike White had gone to war, it might be a Raleigh or a Kool, or a brand called Rameses that seemed to be made of ground Egyptian mummies. Even for these you whimpered gratefully when the candy-store man, after much stalling, loftily brought forth from his secret cache a single pack. It was, his attitude suggested, the very last in the state.

We felt no qualms about cigarettes. Why not smoke? It was good for you. Full-page magazine ads told us in 1937 that "By speeding up the flow of digestive fluids and increasing alkalinity, Camels give digestion a helping hand." And without cigarettes, how were you to express the ineffable? Paul Henreid at the rail of the ship in *Now, Voyager*, lighting two cigarettes at the same time while Bette Davis watches, and handing her one. Lauren Bacall at the door in *To Have and Have Not*: "Anybody got a match?" Bogey, who almost single-handedly turned the cigarette into a swagger stick and defined the niceties of its style.

Beer, in the new 3.2 model, was usually available just off-campus in places like the Purity and the P-Bell. Students drank with slightly more class in New Haven: when the Whiffenpoofs assembled at Mory's with their glasses raised on high, they drank ale, perhaps because it rhymes with Yale. The technology of the beer picnic took a great leap forward with the introduction in 1935 of beer cans. But, as usual, this advance into the future created new problems. Now you *had* to remember to bring a can opener.

Football, of course, was the center of gravity in college sports, the glamorous nucleus around which many elements revolved. Football was usually the college's closest link with its alumni and their pocketbooks, and with the public at large from whom future students (and future budget allocations) would come. For some high school graduates, football scholarships made a college education possible. For the student body at large, football provided pre-game rallies, floats to be made for parades, cheerleading posts to vie for, marching bands

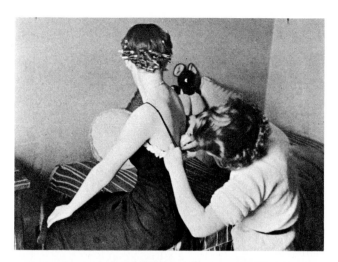

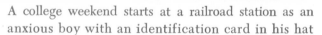

A college weekend starts at a railroad station as an anxious boy with an identification card in his hat looks for his date, and a date waits to be found. The endings are usually happy: dates are united,

to join, the games themselves to attend, the post-game revelry of alumni reunions and fraternity dances. This was the stuff of which "school spirit" was made, a passion that reached fever pitch on the eve of the Big Game.

As Helen Harman, who spent her childhood in California, remembers: "Every year the climax of the football season at the University of California at Berkeley (referred to nationally these days as 'Berkeley' but always called 'Cal' locally) was the Big Game with the college's arch rival, Stanford. Cal's colors are blue and gold, and Stanford's are red and white. Feeling against Stanford annually ran high, and it extended itself to an anti-red-and-white feeling: one year in the late '30s, Cal partisans all over town overturned billboards advertising Chesterfields because they showed eleven football players in red jerseys with white letters spelling THEY SATISFY. Even Berkeley's red fire engines were seized and painted blue and gold so often (much shaking of heads and wondering what the next atrocity of the

younger generation would be) that in 1938 the fire department itself painted the engines blue and gold in honor of Cal's trip to the Rose Bowl.

"On the hills back of Berkeley was (and is, I presume) the 'Big C'—a giant concrete letter, normally painted deep yellow (for gold), visible for miles. As the day of the Big Game approached, Cal students began their night-long vigils with bonfires to keep marauding Stanford students from painting the C red. Some years the Stanford students overwhelmed the guards and the day of the Big Game would dawn with—ultimate disgrace!—a Scarlet Letter on view.

"We used to hike up to the Big C and amuse ourselves by chipping away at the C's strata—first gold, then red, then gold, then red, for *inches*."

Track was less of a national fever than football, but even in track a boy could win a name as well as a letter, especially a boy like Jesse Owens of Ohio State. Like Joe Louis, Jesse was an Alabama boy whose family went North during his childhood. At the Berlin Olympics in

curlers and corsages are skillfully applied and dreamy couples end the evening dancing cheek to cheek.

a young "Okie" whose uprooted family wandered west out of dust-bowl Oklahoma to become migrant fruit-pickers in California. In the "promised land" they were gouged and exploited, harassed by the police and abused by strikebreakers and, in the end, fighting back, Tom Joad killed a man. Robert Jordan—picture him as Gary Cooper if you like—was an idealistic young college professor who died fighting as an American volunteer on the side of the Republic in the Spanish Civil War.

Both characters were drawn from life. Tom's model was an Okie Steinbeck had known. Hemingway's hero was based on Robert Merriman, a young Westerner who had studied economics at the University of Nevada, defended strikers in California and traveled through Russia and Eastern Europe preparing a book, which he never finished, on collective agriculture. He died in Spain as chief of staff of the Abraham Lincoln Battalion of the International Brigades.

To many young Americans the struggles of the Steinbeck and Hemingway heroes seemed noble and inspiring, yet migrant workers remained oppressed and in Spain the Republic fell though some 3,000 Americans had been killed or wounded—extras, it seemed, in a grim dress rehearsal of worse battles to come.

"September 1, 1939"

> I sit in one of the dives
> On Fifty-second Street
> Uncertain and afraid
> As the clever hopes expire
> Of a low dishonest decade. . . .

—W. H. AUDEN

1936, Jesse astounded Adolf Hitler and a stadiumful of Nazis by breaking two world records, matching a third and winning four gold medals.

The mental picture of Jesse Owens returning from Germany to the United States is so tinged with irony that it begs the question: Where was the social conscience of the young in the '30s? Not yet with the Negroes and the Jews, certainly. Sitdowns, not sit-ins, were the order of the day. Concern with religious, ethnic and racial discrimination would come later, in the '40s. Its texts were to be *Native Son, Strange Fruit* and *Gentleman's Agreement*. Its philosophy would be expressed in the title of a popular song which spoke so deeply (if inadvertently) of every American's need, it could be a national anthem: *Don't Fence Me In*.

What did concern young people in the '30s is embodied in the protagonists of two great American novels: Tom Joad of Steinbeck's *The Grapes of Wrath* and Robert Jordan of Hemingway's *For Whom the Bell Tolls*. Tom Joad—or, if you prefer, Henry Fonda—was

If Wallace Stevens was right and all history is modern history, the story of our war, World War II, can never be irrelevant. But it now seems different. In 1940 and 1941 Americans went to Canada, not to escape war but to hasten into it. Some no doubt went for kicks, but for others it was a personal dedication: they wanted to help stop the horror that had spread over Europe: the persecution of the Jews, the blitz of Poland, the humiliation of France, the terrible Battle of Britain, when the whole world held its breath wondering if that handful of men could make it. The United States was not yet in the fight —no one knew for sure if it ever would be—but Canada had joined the Allies in 1939. So young Americans went north and enlisted, some in the glamorous Royal Canadian Air Force, an outfit that had lured their fathers during a similar period in World War I.

And then came Pearl Harbor. In those days in the Navy, if you were black you worked in the mess, period. Mess Attendant Dorie Miller on the battleship *West Virginia* didn't know his place. In the screaming, blazing maelstrom of that Sunday morning at Pearl, Dorie

College offers a chance for a final fling before the plunge into a world turning increasingly uncertain. An outdoor blanket party around a fire is decorously daring. Beer, another great cohesive element of campus life, provides a challenge for champions—an expert chug-a-lugger can empty a hefty stein in a few huge swallows. At football home-coming weekends, social fraternities compete in displays of loyalty to The Team. At Indiana University, Alpha Omicron Pi offers a rousing cancan with a traffic-stopping finale.

found himself on deck. First he moved his badly wounded captain to a safer position. Then Dorie, in his white apron, took over an unmanned, deck-mounted machine gun and fired at the waves of incoming dive bombers until his ammunition ran out and his ship sank. Two years later Dorie Miller went down with the U.S.S. *Liscome Bay* off the Gilbert Islands.

Also in the South Pacific, Lieut. John F. Kennedy led to safety the crew of PT-109 after a Japanese destroyer had cut her in two. Early in the afternoon of November 22, 1963, just over 20 years later, I was walking down Madison Avenue in New York City enjoying the still-pleasant autumn weather. Suddenly I noticed that people were forming little clusters in the street, inclining their heads to listen at open car windows. "Jesus," I heard a man exclaim, "I gotta call my broker!" Most of us remember exactly what we were doing when we heard that Jack Kennedy had been shot. Two of us, Bruce Henderson and Sam Summerlin, have written a

whole book about what people remember of that moment.

He was *our* president, the first born in our century, the youngest man ever elected to the office and, we were sure, certain to be one of the best. We loved him when somebody asked, "How did you become a war hero?" and he answered, "It was absolutely involuntary. They sank my boat."

My high school classmate Robert Coate is now a Californian and active in politics. But in World War II Bob was an Army medic who was captured, shot in the arm by retreating Germans and left for dead. Army doctors eventually saved his arm, but it took a while.

"I spent six months in Army hospitals," he told me. "You may recall Percy Jones Hospital in Battle Creek, Mich. The only people in Percy Jones were nerve injuries and amputees. It is a staggering sight to go into a hospital and see only young men, most of whom are either crippled or have lost limbs.

"About the time I was finally able to move around, Woody Herman's band came to play. My father had told me that a friend of his was in Woody's band playing sax, and I should go say hello to him if I had the chance. Herman played in an auditorium where all of us patients sat. The curtain parted and there was the Herman Herd! They sounded marvelous, great, out of this world. But after about four or five numbers, Herman said, 'I'm very sorry, we have to terminate the program,' and the curtain closed. I thought, I wonder what that was? I went backstage to find the man my father had referred me to. All of Herman's band were just numbly moving around, packing their instruments. I found my man and asked him what had happened. 'You can't imagine what it's like,' he said. 'From where we were sitting on that stage, we could see two thousand young guys, all without legs and arms.' And he said, 'I don't know how we played even four numbers.'"

Herbert Spohn, now a psychologist at the Menninger Foundation in Topeka, came to this country in 1936 as a German refugee kid of 12. He had, inevitably, a very special perspective on World War II, partly the result of his first experiences here:

"America seemed immense in every way, in promise and in disappointment. At first, the very atmosphere seemed to say, Anything is possible, any wish, hope, dream, can be fulfilled, any preference or whim indulged. Shortly after I arrived, I entered a soap-company-sponsored contest in which you had to match a set of photographs of twins. Such contests were very popular during those Depression years because the grand prize was always some vast, unimaginably great amount of cash. It seems to me the contest I entered promised a million dollars. Even if the amount is inflated by memory, it matches my then anticipations of America.

"Within a week after entering, a thick envelope ad-

War comes to Yale when sandbags are piled among the ivy against air raids. Girls step into men's jobs in steel mills (*opposite page, top*) and into women's jobs by marrying servicemen, sometimes in mass ceremonies like the one advertised at right and pictured below.

dressed to me from the soap company arrived. My God, here it was—I had won a million dollars—only in America!—the envelope was thick with hundred-dollar bills! And of course it wasn't. They had sent further instructions for more puzzles to be completed and more soap wrappers to be sent in. Yet notwithstanding the impact of reality upon my great expectations, some sense and hope of unlimited possibilities for self-development and self-aggrandizement, some sense that nothing was fixed, irrevocable, pre-ordained in America remained with me well into my 30s and beyond."

As a youth, Spohn struggled to gain acceptance from his American schoolmates but did not really begin to feel like an American until after combat service in the U.S. Army in World War II.

"World War II was the great enterprise of my generation," he said. "It fixed in me another image of America that remains largely uneroded by subsequent events. I remember an enormous tank retriever truck rumbling fully loaded with a disabled tank through a small French town, setting the earth over which it rolled and all the nearby houses trembling. That vignette symbolized for me American armed might in World War II as something inexorable, massive, inevitably victorious. And it was good to be a part of it, to be entitled to be identified with it."

There were others who served. Sergeant X of the beautiful story "For Esmé—with Love and Squalor," a

man very much like his creator, J. D. Salinger. And Yossarian, the too-sane madman of *Catch-22* who bore a remarkable resemblance to Joseph Heller and like him was a bombardier with the Air Force in the Italian campaign. Prewitt, whose bugle I can almost hear still, blowing out of the pages of *From Here to Eternity*, who will always wear for me the haunted face of Montgomery Clift. And of course Kilroy. Kilroy the ubiquitous turned up in every theater of the war, and found a postwar home in Tennessee Williams' play *Camino Real*. His finest moment came at the Potsdam conference in the summer of 1945. A special V.I.P. latrine had been set up there for the Big Three, and despite the iron vigilance of its guards, Joseph Stalin was heard to inquire of his American interpreter, as he came out, "Who is Kilroy?"

What did *you* do in the war, Mommy? In the summer of 1942 Mommy worked for the Volunteer Land Corps on a farm in Vermont, mowing hay and milking. Helen Harman became a welder on the swing shift at the Albina shipyard in Portland, Ore., turning out LCIs and LSTs. I worked on the night shift in a Richmond factory, inspecting airplane piston rings, and the summer of 1944 is in memory an almost surrealistic blend of tanned young men in crisp uniforms, home on their last leave; the thundering drone of the plant, like the motors of airplanes that six months hence might be carrying these very friends; and outside the factory, moonlight on the alfalfa fields. Late in the war Joyce Furgie, from the Mississippi river town of Moline, Ill., joined the Red Cross and served in Korea and Japan. She is one of the last (and among the few) members of our generation to see the fabled city of Peking.

Mecca, New Hampshire

Mecca beckoned. Not, of course, the real Mecca to which Malcolm X's amazing life-journey did take him near the end, but closer Meccas like New York and California. Robert Zang and Benjamin Gim, friends and classmates at West High School in Salt Lake City, were typical of many. After the Army and Columbia Law School, they did not go back to Utah but took a coast apiece—Bob went to San Francisco, Benny stayed in Manhattan. New York was also my destination, but a girl from the sticks knew better than to go there directly; an oblique approach was called for. And so, with several of my sorority sisters, I got a job as one of the waitress corps at the Hanover Inn.

The village of Hanover, N.H., which I saw first on a June day in 1946, seemed pure enchantment, the quintessential New England I had learned to love on calendars. Beside it, at the bottom of the hill, flowed the noble Connecticut River. To the east was a "mountain," the first I had ever really seen; I looked out the window every day on arising, to make sure it was still there. The

Swept off her feet (*above*) by a sailor and by the news of the surrender of Japan, a girl in Miami wholeheartedly joins in the nationwide jubilation over the end of World War II, the Swing Generation's war. Others, in the picture below, celebrate in Chicago.

Inn itself was a fine hostelry that breathed comfort and tradition. My cup overflowed when one morning I found myself serving breakfast to a solitary Robert Frost. I did my utmost not to let his poached egg slither off the toast as I lowered it before him with trembling arm.

Happily the rumor was true

Opposite the Inn was the campus of Dartmouth, indeed we were part of Dartmouth, one of the handsomest of New England colleges. Dartmouth once had (perhaps still has) the reputation of developing wild men, up there in the snowy wastes, and it was said that when stray girls wandered into range, Dartmouth came down like the wolf on the fold. Happily, this rumor turned out to be true.

Our eight months at Dartmouth may not seem a typical experience, but in two ways it was. First because it provided the sort of collegiate frolic that the war had cheated us of, and which we still wanted. (There was the difference that now, between parties, we were waiting on tables instead of cracking books.) Second because it was, for us, the opening chapter in an ever recurring American initiation rite: seeing our country, this unbelievable country, more than ever a brave new world with such wonders and people in it we could hardly wait to see them all.

Hanover was a fine place to start. Here we encountered our first really great art, the Orozco frescoes on the walls of Dartmouth's library. Here we were taken, by some of the wild men, to see the studio of the sculptor Saint-Gaudens in the foothills of the White Mountains nearby. Here for the first time we square-danced for real, at a little out-of-the-way village up the river. Here for the first time we met truly exotic Americans like Eedu and Anneliese Suursoo, two handsome blonds in their 20s who had abandoned Europe for America but still carried about them a certain aura that was unfamiliar and impressive. Eedu had literally lost his country: he had been an Estonian, a seaman, and Estonia had disappeared into the U.S.S.R. Anneliese had been German, but now her country was wherever Eedu was. Eedu was like some beautiful, dazed animal recovering from a near-mortal blow—he still knew very little English and was usually silent—and Anneliese was both wife and shepherd. She was as smart as she was good-looking, about our age and a thousand years older. Christmas Eve they invited us to their tiny Hanover apartment and we never forgot that great evergreen tree trimmed only with lighted white candles, and the black bread, spread with butter, that Anneliese had found or somehow made for a taste of home. I think we sang carols as we sat in the candlelight, but I know Eedu did not sing, and I tried unsuccessfully to read in his eyes what he was thinking.

Of all the frolics, Winter Carnival was the most fun,

with a deserved notoriety as the foremost of Eastern college saturnalia. We probably did not do it justice in 1947, however. A great percentage of Dartmouth men were veterans not long home, and many of the veterans were ex-Marines. After three or four years of outdoor living in places like Bougainville and Iwo Jima, their enthusiasm for fresh air had waned, and a vigorous sporting life did not attract them nearly so much as a fraternity house game room with lots of booze and girls. Dartmouth men had long since run through the 10,000 gallons of New England rum that Eleazar Wheelock brought into the wilderness; now they were drinking "Seabreezes"—gin and grapefruit juice—by the pitcherful, and turning the music up loud. Maybe it was the freshmen who made those impressive ice sculptures that dotted the campus and who took part in all those ski events.

Twelve o'clock struck, the party was over, it was time to grow up. Ginny Hoyler and I found ourselves in Manhattan, Ginny working for the Community Service Society, conducting troops of slum kids through the New York subways to distant dental clinics. New York subways are much like the Surinam jungle, but Ginny with Wolverine cunning doped out a system: she hung back and let the kids lead the way. Some infallible instinct told them which exit to take and what direction to turn.

I enrolled in what might be called the finishing school of Miss Content Peckham, chief of research at *Time* Magazine. She ran a possibly nonaccredited institution of higher learning, but a good one. I suppose I had dreamed of resembling Jane Wyman in *The Lost Weekend*, the best-looking researcher *Time* never had; in memory, at least, Jane wears one divine little number after another, with never a stocking seam crooked or a hair out of place. It didn't work out quite that way. On the other hand, none of my friends were drunks, at least not steadily.

The usual solace

The Swing Era was nearing its end. The natural sweetness of youth was laced now with bitter flavors. The Bomb and the gas ovens had left an acrid taste we would never fully get rid of. And we had heard the Iron Curtain descending; Winston Churchill made us hear it, in his speech at Fulton, Mo., in 1946.

We solaced ourselves in the usual way. Oona O'Neill married Charlie Chaplin; her look-alike and friend, Gloria Vanderbilt, married Leopold Stokowski. Artie Shaw married Ava Gardner. Judy Garland married Vincente Minnelli. After 24 kissless Westerns together, Roy Rogers and Dale Evans got hitched. Even Elizabeth Taylor, that nice little girl that everybody had liked so much in *National Velvet* in 1944, was suddenly old enough to have dates, and it was clearly not going to be long before somebody got her to the altar.

If you weren't deafened by wedding bells, you stood

a good chance of crippling yourself stumbling over baby carriages and strollers. The birth rate took off like a V-2 rocket. Everybody bought Dr. Benjamin Spock's *Pocket Book of Baby and Child Care*. The Age of Spock had begun.

We were crossing several watersheds in the entertainment world. Television was about to take over the American living room. In 1948 there were still only 975,000 sets, but people without sets found reasons to drop in on their more fortunate neighbors when it was time for Milton Berle or Ed Sullivan. The Big Bands were breaking up: as early as 1946, eight bands called it quits within a few weeks of each other. On records, singers were taking the place of the bands, and the industry as a whole was adjusting to the introduction, in 1948, of the long-playing record.

The nation was changing in other ways. The Pennsylvania Turnpike and the Merritt Parkway, the country's first high-speed, long-distance, controlled-access super-

Back at Princeton and other colleges, ex-servicemen display Nazi flags as well as pennants and T-shirts.

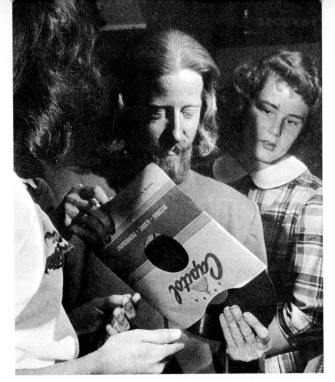

A hippie ahead of his time, bearded Eden Ahbez, a yoga and health-food devotee, displays a record of *Nature Boy*, his 1948 hit song praising the simple life.

highways, had opened in 1940 and now there were more and more of us to crowd such highways: medical breakthroughs like penicillin were keeping us alive longer.

A great change was under way in baseball, presaging vast changes throughout society. In 1947 Jackie Robinson joined the Brooklyn Dodgers, an event which we all recognized as the crossing of an important frontier. Jackie was the first Negro to play in the Major Leagues. It was tough going at first—he was routinely insulted and sometimes even spiked in certain ballparks—but Jackie was tough himself. He became the Rookie of the Year and, two years later, the National League's most valuable player.

The first hippie appeared around 1948. His name was Eden Ahbez and he wrote a song called *Nature Boy*, about someone like himself. Eden was a gentle person who believed in love and ate vegetables. I was among the millions who found Nat King Cole's recording of his song irresistible.

At about the same time, Allen Ginsberg was kicked out of Columbia for scrawling an obscene, anti-Semitic phrase on his dormitory window. Ginsberg is a complex man, and it seems clear from his subsequent life and work—*e.g.*, the poem *Kaddish*, an elegy for his mother —that his love for his traditional-Jewish origins is at least as great as his impatience was then. Even then Ginsberg was trying to find—as we were all trying to find—a way of life that would work, and feel right. Interestingly, Ginsberg attempted a clean-shaven, white-collar, 9 to 5 existence in San Francisco for two years as a market research consultant. And he found it was not for him. He has become a good poet, but it may turn out

that his life is his major work. The critic Louis Simpson recently concluded, surveying the '60s, "Hemingway created the life-style of the Lost Generation; Ginsberg created that of the Beat. It was a spectacular achievement." He is, of course, the guru of today's turned-on youth. A young friend astounded me recently, first by saying that she adores Frank Sinatra (I adored Frank myself, but that was 20 years ago), second by adding that on her campus now, Allen Ginsberg would outdraw Sinatra any day.

What will the Big Picture be?

The puzzle we started on, way back then, has become very complicated. It is still unfinished and spreads farther all the time. Who can say what the Big Picture will be? Meanwhile I'm keeping my eye on Robert Rauschenberg (b. 1925, raised in Port Arthur, Texas), who like all good artists seems to pick up hints of the future a little ahead of the rest of us.

If I saw a Rauschenberg work in the Sahara, I think I could tell it was by an American and my contemporary. He is above all the master puzzler, trying to find a way to make disparate things fit together harmoniously. He likes to combine past and present, the divine and the mundane, the funny and the serious, painting with sculpture, real objects with representations. Somehow his artist's vision makes them coexist. The objects in his paintings are probably symbols, but they are themselves too. In *Tracer*, a lush Rubens nude may represent nostalgia for the past and for traditional concepts of order and beauty. On the other hand, Rauschenberg obviously enjoys her just as a lovely and desirable woman. A bald eagle on a perch says, perhaps, that the American spirit is immobilized; the eagle is also there because Rauschenberg loves animals. The painting was made back in 1964, but already the artist sensed the increasing burden of the Vietnam war and the problem of the cities. He even suggests—in the caged songbirds—our corruption of the physical environment. It cannot be accidental that the painting (reproduced here in black and white) is red, white, blue and black.

Whatever the Big Picture itself turns out to be, there is a name for those of us who added our pieces to it in the '30s and '40s. We are the Swing Generation—not only for the music we loved and still love, but because, like the swing shift in those wartime factories, we were the pivot between two worlds.

—JOAN SWALLOW REITER

Rauschenberg's *Tracer*, says author Joan Reiter in the text above, shows new pieces of the big picture puzzle which the young of the Swing Era are still solving.

The Men Who Made the Music:
Glenn Miller

It is ironic that, more than a quarter century after his disappearance over the English Channel, this angular and schoolmasterish man still is a symbol of romance for millions of people. For despite the evocative bittersweetness of the ballads his band played during those long-ago evenings of the late '30s and early '40s, despite the insouciant lilt of his *Jersey Bounce*, the unaffectedly high spirits of his *Chattanooga Choo Choo*, he looked like a psalm-singing choirmaster, standing there on the bandstand with his tight-lipped, perfunctory smile.

Of personal appearances, he once said: "I'm so nervous I'd rather go to jail than make one."

It is preposterous that so long after his passing this man's name should recall to so many what were to them the best of times. But such is the music of Alton Glenn Miller, out of Clarinda, Iowa, into the big time, for a few brief years the most successful of all big band leaders and last seen on Dec. 15, 1944 as he left England on a flight for Paris.

Part of the secret of the immortal Miller mystique lies in the emotions his music and his band expressed which the leader seemed to lack. A "Glenn Miller Band" under a Ray McKinley, a Tex Beneke, a Buddy De Franco is still a draw while other honored names call up only nostalgic echoes. He was *the* giant in the days of his glory—playing summertimes at Glen Island Casino while a nation listened beside radios in the dusk; playing autumns and winters in New York at the Hotel Pennsylvania's Cafe Rouge and other dance tabernacles of the period; playing at all times and places through the portable phonographs which were part of every picnic basket and through the jukeboxes he correctly credited with

Miller supplies all the brass as he and fellow Colorado University summer students play in pianist Holly Moyer's band in 1925. Sax

starting him toward success. At least every other tune he recorded was an anthem of the age—and of the eminent bandleaders of the era, he was among the less dramatic.

Yet the creative process is part of the personality of the artist; and the Miller Sound, for all its twanging of the emotions, probably could not have emanated from a man unlike Glenn Miller. As a bandstand personality, Miller stood well back in the shade of colorful leaders whose philosophies and life styles shaped their dance bands in the '30s and early '40s: Goodman, a man of great, great style, unfailingly articulate and authoritative; Artie Shaw, quixotic, connubial, the catalyst of an infinity of gossip-column items; Tommy Dorsey, a brawling, damn-the-torpedoes broth of an Irishman who could be a real son of a bitch but almost never an uncharming one.

Miller had his orchestra, his genius as an arranger and his tremendous organizational and administrative ability. It was all he needed. He was then and still is more popular than Goodman, Shaw or Dorsey. Off the stand, he had, so far as I could tell, practically no personality at all. He had friends who spoke warmly of his very positive character, wild sense of humor and interest in the world around him. They extolled his devotion to music and his help to other musicians. In the half-dozen or so conversations I had with him over about four years, I found Miller perfectly civil but almost implausibly perfunctory and staggeringly uninformed about (and seemingly indifferent to) practically everything —except his music.

"Stylization in music is inevitable," Barry Ulanov, jazz historian and critic, quotes Miller as saying. "The style is the man. . . . Would you say that Wagner wasn't stylized? Is Ravel criticized for being Ravel?"

Of his devotion to music there is no question. He knew his trade and insisted on perfection in its practice. "We not only rehearse arrangements," one of his sidemen once said, "we rehearse every bar a thousand times until he's satisfied."

Nobody ever questioned, either, his warm devotion to his wife Helen and their two adopted children, though Miller never saw the little daughter, Jonnie, who joined the family after he went overseas. Paul Tanner, a former Miller trombonist, says Miller was interested in the world around him, but other old associates, pressed to describe Miller's outside interests, could recall only that he played golf and the stock market, both better than most musicians. (Bassist Trigger Alpert once asked Miller what to do with his savings. "Buy AT&T," said Miller. "What's AT&T?" asked Trigger.)

But, oh, his music

Even close and admiring associates say Miller's attitude toward most things was strictly business. He was not rare among bandleaders of the era in having struggled up from poverty entirely on his own merits, but where others blossomed into some of the most colorful characters of the age, Miller, though no small-town hick, retained many of the values of Clarinda, Iowa.

Permit me to anticipate critics (including some who were very close to him) who may say that I did not know Miller very well. Indeed, I did not, but what matters, really, is how Miller impressed the millions of people who clustered in front of his various bandstands. Many of them have told me that he impressed them as—well, as a nice fellow who didn't have much to say but who was perfectly pleasant. But, oh, his music—and then they rave about the sound that enchanted them in the evenings when their world was young.

Miller was born in Clarinda, Iowa, on the first of March 1904 to a poor family which moved steadily westward dur-

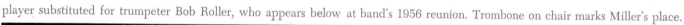

player substituted for trumpeter Bob Roller, who appears below at band's 1956 reunion. Trombone on chair marks Miller's place.

A natty, mustached Miller stands leftmost in a poolside picture taken in the summer of 1934 at the Sands Point, N.Y. Beach Club where the newly formed Dorsey Brothers Orchestra was then playing. Half the band were people who had come east along with Miller, vainly seeking jobs in Billy Rose's Casino de Paree. They included vocalist Kay Weber, here flanked by co-leaders Tommy (*at left*) and Jimmy, and drummer Ray McKinley (*third from left*). Miller left the Dorseys in 1935 to assemble an orchestra for British bandleader Ray Noble, at the piano in the picture below. Miller, now clean-shaven, stands in rear center between trumpeter Charlie Spivak (*left*) and saxophonist Bud Freeman.

ing his childhood. His father was a carpenter and contractor who had a hard time supporting a family of six. For a time the family lived in a sod hut in North Platte, Neb. Glenn got his first trombone from a butcher who employed him as an errand boy. "It wasn't much of a one," said Glenn, "but it got me into the school band."

He had a passionate interest in music—on his own terms. He took no music courses at the University of Colorado while putting himself through school for two years by playing in a college band. But ten years later he studied on his own with the noted theorist Professor Joseph Schillinger, and one of his greatest hits, *Moonlight Serenade*, grew out of an arranging exercise he wrote for Schillinger. Miller never stopped learning and experimenting. He used his Army Air Forces Band as a laboratory and was planning a postwar civilian band with a new sound.

The teen-age college dropout played with several small bands, recorded a little with such jazz giants as Bix Beiderbecke and the Mound City Blue Blowers, sold an arrangement for $50 to Roger Wolfe Kahn, a scion of great wealth and a hopeless swing addict, and made the varsity, so to speak, when Ben Pollack hired him in 1925. In the late '20s and early '30s the Pollack band, firmly based on the leader's solid drumming and Miller's arrangements, had more authentic jazz feeling than any other white group. Pollack was a gifted leader with an uncanny ear for talent and his various bands included, along with Miller, such expressive soloists as Bud Freeman on tenor saxophone, Jack Teagarden on trombone, Benny Goodman on clarinet and Jimmy McPartland and Harry James on trumpet. In 1925, when the 16-year-old Goodman joined Pollack, he and Miller formed a friendship that lasted all Glenn's life.

Later, when Benny was being widely accused of rapidly outgrowing his hat, Miller, a man not noted for overpraising his acquaintances, said: "I roomed with him . . . he was a swell gent then and he still is . . . . You've got to really know Benny to appreciate his many wonderful qualities." Goodman later recalled Miller as "an excellent friend—generous and concerned . . . all the musicians in our circle admired him tremendously."

The abiding image that haunted and still haunts a whole generation is of Miller the leader. But musicians view things a little differently and, while not disdaining that side of Miller, they speak more admiringly of his talents as an organizer, an arranger and a jazz trombonist. When he could get the sidemen he wanted, Miller organized fine bands, as he did for the Dorsey Brothers, Ray Noble and himself. His own success with his very commercial swing was predicated principally on his own arrangements. And it is accolade enough to state that in a gutbucket time, when trombonists like Jack Teagarden, Jimmy Harrison, Lawrence Brown, Miff Mole, "Tricky Sam" Nanton and Benny Morton were abroad in the land, Glenn Miller did them no disservice when he kept their company. He was marvelous in a lovely, lyrical way, his slide slipping langorously from position to position to weave a pattern of pure jazz.

Miller was never dazzled by his own skill as a trombonist, perhaps recalling that in Texas in the '20s he failed to get into the Jimmy Joy band because he couldn't play the kind of trombone Jimmy wanted. "If I could play as well as Tommy Dorsey," Glenn once told his wife, "I'd star myself and others in the band. But since I can't play as well as Tommy, I'll have to make the band great by arrangements and precision playing."

"I think he would have traded in the whole thing," said Miller's treasured trumpeter Bobby Hackett, "to be able to play like Jack Teagarden or Tommy Dorsey." Yet he showed little professional jealousy and once wrote special music and lyrics to *Basin Street Blues* for Teagarden to sing.

Precision he demanded. "Order, proportion, planning, those were central to Glenn Miller's function as a bandleader," says Ulanov.

"In a field that was notoriously casual," says jazz critic John S. Wilson, "Mr. Miller was a systematic and painstaking man."

The right socks and cigarettes

He saw to it that others shared his pains. When the Miller band was on the Chesterfield show, sidemen who smoked had to smoke Chesterfields. Everybody had to wear maroon socks. "It was always 'Get your suits pressed and stop talking on the bandstand and shape up,'" a former sideman has recalled.

Miller wanted to be proud of whatever band he played with. He was content to earn $12 a week or so playing and arranging for Smith Ballew in the early '30s, but when the band played Denver, Miller refused to appear. His home was in nearby Boulder and he did not wish to be seen by people he knew with a band no better than Ballew's. "The band wasn't that bad," said Ray McKinley, who did play the Denver date. "It just wasn't good."

McKinley also remembered a story told by Hal Dicken-

Miller fishing, with wife Helen (in neckerchief) and friends.

Glenn "holds" Washington Monument in wife's 1940 gag shot.

son, one of the singers who made up Miller's Modernaires. The band was playing its theme song to start a concert in a big auditorium. The curtain rose. Glenn walked to the center microphone to greet the audience but on the way noticed that Hal displayed no handkerchief in the breast pocket of his jacket. Miller took a spare handkerchief from his own inside breast pocket, tucked it into Hal's outside pocket, walked back to the mike, turned, and said to Hal, "We wear handkerchiefs in this orchestra, Mr. Dickenson."

McKinley quotes Dickenson as saying, "To this day I don't even go to the bathroom without a handkerchief."

To capture the crowd

Miller fired men for failing to measure up to his standards but never for tossing a really inspired impromptu jazz riff into an arrangement. He played commercial music but he appreciated good jazz and had been a good jazzman.

"He was deeply concerned to find richer harmonic resources for jazz and dance bands, separately and together," says Ulanov. "He was convinced that in jazz, 'for the sake of rhythm, harmony was forgotten.'"

"I don't want to be the king of swing or anything else," Miller said one evening in 1939. "I'd rather have a reputation as one of the best all-round bands."

I think he had *the* best all-round band. But long before that, while he was with Pollack, he played some good jazz with Goodman and others, and there is testimony to his ability as a hot trombonist on a number of discs released in the years immediately thereafter. My own favorite is a 12-inch Brunswick by Red Nichols of *Sally Won't You Come Back*, on which he plays a beautiful, lazy obbligato behind Teagarden's vocal that is as memorable for me as any Armstrong ever played behind Bessie Smith. Yet he never allowed his affinity for jazz to turn his head and he was ever mindful of what captured the crowd.

"He had the ability to know what the public would like," Chuck Gentry, a former Miller saxophonist, remembers. "Occasionally he'd ask the band what numbers they liked. Whatever we liked, he would reject, thinking that whatever musicians liked the public wouldn't—and he was right."

He did not pander to commercialism—his taste was impeccable and his integrity irreproachable—but his intuition amounted to genius. Not only did he infuse the Pollack band with freshness, but he made arrangements of *Basin Street Blues* and *Beale Street Blues* which were used for a recording date, in February 1931, by a Goodman pickup group and which were the first things truly in the style Goodman had been trying to develop. Subsequently he provided the Dorsey Brothers with the idiom that made their band distinctive. And soon after that he hit upon what was to become known as the Miller Sound.

This discovery came in 1935 when Ray Noble, a British bandleader whose recordings had become best sellers because of their extraordinary resonance, commissioned Miller to form a group for him to lead during a forthcoming engagement at the Rainbow Room in New York. He could not have chosen an abler surrogate; Miller's taste and knowledge of musicians' capabilities produced a superb personnel. But Miller's association with Noble was important because of something else. In the Noble band, trumpeter Peewee

Erwin played the lead an octave above the tenor saxophone lead. Erwin left and his replacement proved less strong-lipped; Miller imaginatively substituted a clarinet lead.

This was the basis of the famous Miller Sound, though there is more to it than just a clarinet lead, as Ray McKinley has explained: "You also have to pick a key that will keep your clarinet way up high and your altos just about as high as they can play and you've got to keep the harmony tight. To get that shimmering sound the reeds must employ vibrato and have to be voiced close together and very high."

The Miller Sound did not particularly appeal to Noble and was not much used by the Noble band, but Miller must have sensed its possibilities, and it may have helped spur Miller to launch his own band in 1937. It was not a leap to be made lightly, despite the temptations of fame, the excitement and the challenge. When Goodman, Shaw, the Dorseys, Miller and others decided to form big bands in the '30s they took a tremendous financial risk. These musicians had assurances of work in radio and recording studios amounting practically to annuities, and some quite brilliant performers failed as bandleaders. Miller could have grown rich in comfort arranging and playing trombone for others, and for two impoverished, despairing years of indifferent audiences, snowbound buses and shortages of competent musicians he may have wished he had stayed in the studios. But to stay in the studios in the '30s was to acknowledge a measure of insecurity, a lack of ambition. Miller was not given to such acknowledgements.

We tend to recall the '30s, as we lived them or heard about them, as the Swing Era when Goodman was God to the kids shagging in the aisles of the Paramount Theater. It was a golden time of big bands playing in the great hotels of New York, Kansas City, Chicago, San Francisco and Boston, a time of theme songs, each with an imprimatur immediately identifiable, a time of solo vocalists and all those cozy singing groups sitting at the side of the bandstand and then rising, when summoned, like robots, stepping smartly to stage center to inform us that they hadn't the slightest intention of ever smiling again. It was a time of ballrooms and lakeside dance pavilions with magic names like Glen Island Casino and Frank Dailey's Meadowbrook, a time of broadcasts "coming direct to you from. . . ." It was the best of times but, for those in the business, only after they had made it.

Jet-black toast and tough rehearsals

A novitiate could be nasty and the early odyssey of Glenn Miller could not have been more discouraging, as a movie, *The Glenn Miller Story*, later showed, though its fictions and cloying sentimentality somewhat obscure the real Miller.

"Nothing I saw in the movie made sense except the music," said the late Hal McIntyre who, off and on, roomed with Miller from 1937 to 1941, was one of the most durable of his sidemen and got Miller's financial backing when he started his own band. "They made Glenn into a warm, human sort of fellow. He was the coldest fish that ever lived. I knew him better than anyone except maybe his mother. I know how he brushed his teeth in the morning and how he liked his toast. The waiter would bring up the toast and Glenn would put that icy eye on it and say, 'Take that toast back and bring it back jet black.' The poor waiter is standing

Wilbur Schwartz, Glenn's favorite lead clarinetist, who helped produce the distinctive Miller Sound, solos during one of the band's first recording sessions for Bluebird in April 1939. By the end of that year, the success of his records on jukeboxes, like the one on which Miller leans affectionately below, had made him America's top swing musician.

there, not knowing what it's all about, and Glenn would get impatient and ask, 'How dumb can you get?'

"I've seen him break up a rehearsal when things weren't going right and point: 'You and you and you—and you. You're fired.' Just like that. I'm the only guy who could get along with him. He was a miserable man. And he was my buddy. I loved the guy."

When Miller began recruiting musicians in 1937 he found few as good as McIntyre. In retrospect, one wonders if his band was worth much more than the $200 it got in June for an 8 p.m. to 3 a.m. appearance at Playland Casino in Rye, N.Y. But in the same month the band was booked for two weeks at the Blue Room of the Roosevelt in New Orleans, where it stayed for 10, and from there it went to the Adolphus in Dallas and the Nicollet in Minneapolis. The band created little public excitement and Miller struggled constantly to improve it, weeding out drunks and dubs among his sidemen.

He got a few coast-to-coast broadcasts, but after a disastrous tour through blizzard-swept Pennsylvania he gave up the band. In March of 1938, however, he began to rebuild. To a nucleus of McIntyre, Chummy MacGregor (piano), Rolly Bundock (bass) and Bob Price (trumpet), he added clarinetist Wilbur Schwartz, drummer Bob Spangler, trumpeter Johnny Austin and tenor saxophonist Tex Beneke.

"I drove all night through a snowstorm to New York," said Beneke later, "and when I walked into the studio where Miller was rehearsing I thought he'd give me some sack time. But he only said, 'Hello, there, Tex, grab your horn and let's go.' "

A little later Glenn hired Ray Eberle, a singer without professional experience, and in September Marion Hutton joined him. But at this point nothing seemed to help. In February 1939 he was close to giving up again, but despite lack of public acclaim, his music was catching the ear of people who knew a coming thing when they heard it. On his 35th birthday he was signed to play all summer at the Glen Island Casino. Summer was three months away, but he had caught the glory train and had more offers for immediate gigs than he could accept. One was too good to resist—a stretch at Frank Dailey's Meadowbrook ballroom in New Jersey. Glenn would lose money but gain 10 broadcasts a week in an age when air exposure could make a band overnight. And by then he was proud of his band. Drummer Maurice Purtill, lured away from a flourishing teaching career, was invigorating the rhythm section and there was a new guitarist. Glenn added another trumpet and a trombone and had the first big band with eight brass.

Crowd in Hotel Pennsylvania's Cafe Rouge stands too entranced to dance as brass men wave "wah-wah" derbies in unison.

The Meadowbrook and the Glen Island engagements were prodigiously successful, carrying the Miller Sound to every corner of the country. Now the band could reap the bonanza. At the Baltimore Hippodrome it drew $19,000, the biggest theater gross in the city's history, and in Syracuse it attracted the largest crowd ever to attend a dance there. For Bluebird that summer it recorded *Little Brown Jug* and its biggest hit, *In the Mood*.

Dancing derbies and discernible tunes

By now the band had an unmistakable individuality. There was the riff repeated over and over, swelling, then fading, and finally returning in a shattering crescendo. The astute Miller had picked up from Jimmie Lunceford the trick of having the brass section wave its "wah-wah" derbies in unison. Some sidemen said they felt like clowns, but the crowds liked it. And there was, of course, The Sound.

"Though his arrangements are inventive and refreshing," said the New York *Times* in January 1940, "he never forgets the melodic line. He lets you recognize the tune." People liked that, too.

The band was working some 100 hours a week now, recording an average of two sides a week and appearing on radio for Chesterfield cigarettes thrice weekly. In early 1940 it was appearing not only at the Hotel Pennsylvania's Cafe Rouge but on the stage at the Paramount Theater. Not every disc was a hit. Miller took the pop tunes of the day as they came, and some were dreadful, but Miller could put his gloss even on something like *When Paw Was Courtin' Maw*. If his upbeat recordings of *I'll Never Smile Again* failed in competition against Tommy Dorsey's version, his *Tuxedo Junction* handily beat Erskine Hawkins at his own tune.

The band made a couple of inoffensive movies, *Sun Valley Serenade* and *Orchestra Wives* of which TIME said, "Glenn Miller acts like Glenn Miller, without too much discredit to Glenn Miller." Nobody could make Glenn act, but the films were successful, since the band seemed beyond blunders. It monotonously won just about every conceivable popularity poll. Three teen-age girls in Philadelphia, listening raptly on a summer evening to a recording of Miller's *Moonlight Serenade*, failed to observe a fire in the house until a fireman rushed in to put it out. Even sidemen who hated him enjoyed the band's prestige. "There was excitement," said a contemporary. "They were on top."

And then, suddenly and shockingly and very, very sadly it came to an end on the evening of Sept. 27, 1942 at the Central Theater in Passaic, N.J., while Marion Hutton sobbed uncontrollably. The band had spent most of that last day together in a saloon across from the theater, and by the time one trumpeter was supposed to climb down the tiers in which the band was arranged on stage and take his solo he was too drunk to move. "Okay," said Miller, "stay up there, you son of a bitch."

Most of the sidemen were already slated for the armed services. Miller, who was 38, married, a father and weak-eyed, could have escaped the draft until the German army reached Chicago. He enlisted, was given a commission in the Army Air Forces and started organizing another band.

Higher brass chilled Captain Miller's dream of hatching a clutch of high-class service bands, but he did organize the

Glenn leads band for a studio broadcast. Singers Marion Hutton and the Modernaires surround a microphone *(left)*.

418th Army Air Forces Band out of the pick of a slew of able-bodied former ornaments of symphony orchestras, recording studios and such bands as those of Benny Goodman, Artie Shaw, Harry James, Tommy Dorsey, Will Bradley, Jan Savitt, Vaughn Monroe and Glenn Miller. Out of them he formed a dance band, a pseudosymphonic band with strings, and a controversial marching band.

Miller played *St. Louis Blues* and *Blues in the Night* at march tempo for the drills of the air cadets at Yale University where the band was stationed. The commandant of cadets and others objected. Miller prevailed, however, and even took to swinging Sousa marches, thus bringing to a boil Edwin Franko Goldman, prestigious conductor of Central Park Mall concerts. "It's a disgrace!" fumed Goldman. "No one can improve on a Sousa march. . . . My God!" Marshall Bartholomew, conductor of the Yale Glee Club under whose window the band marched twice daily, said he thought the arrangements were fine. Miller himself responded to Goldman as he usually did to critics.

"There hasn't been a successful Army band in the country," he said, "and if someone doesn't get after band music

and streamline it, Army music will be extinct in another couple of years. We've got to keep pace with the soldiers. They want up-to-date music. Why, there's no question about it—anybody can improve on Sousa."

"It was a marvelous experience," said Peanuts Hucko, remembering how he learned to play clarinet in that band. Peanuts was a tenor saxophonist whom Will Bradley had fired for his inability to play clarinet. Miller said, "You'll play clarinet—that's an order." Peanuts became a highly successful clarinetist.

"Everybody kept playing above their heads," Peanuts said, remembering some great performances recorded on V Discs, that marvelous series of records made, without pay, by a host of top musicians and distributed throughout the armed forces, along with portable phonographs, for the entertainment of the troops. "We made a V Disc of *Stealin' Apples* and it was the most-stolen record of any V Disc. When we got back, they were selling it under the counter for twenty bucks."

Cold and stiff, as he often seemed in real life, Miller confronts Sonja Henie and John Payne in a scene from the 1941 movie *Sun Valley Serenade*. Warm and relaxed was the way Jimmy Stewart played Glenn in the heart-tugging 1954 film *The Glenn Miller Story*, with June Allyson as Helen. The picture drew sobs from some *(bottom)*, snorts from others.

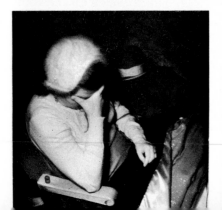

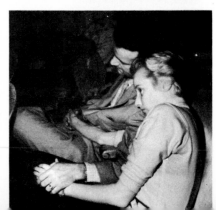

The responsibilities of command did not noticeably erode Miller's disciplinary standards. He occasionally pulled rank on sidemen as though he were still paying them, and he banned mustaches on enlisted men, to the dismay of some brass players who felt that the hair strengthened not only their egos but the brass man's most vital feature—his lip.

"He used to make us toe the mark," said Peanuts. "He said, 'You're musicians but you're also soldiers.' We went along with that—haircut, shoeshine. The GIs we came in contact with appreciated that."

"It killed our souls to have to cut our hair," said Chuck Gentry, "but Miller had his reasons. The band was doing so many unmilitary things that Miller felt we should conform where it was easy. A lot of the guys went out to have uniforms tailor-made. Glenn relegated them to the closet."

"But though Glenn was strict," said McKinley, "sometimes to the point of heartlessness, that was not true when you got right down to the nitty-gritty."

Miller liked Trigger Alpert, got him a draft deferment,

A starchy, jeep-borne Captain Miller appears with bassist Trigger Alpert and drummer Frank Ippolito for a 1943 performance in the Yale Bowl by the 418th Army Air Forces Band. Below, Drum Major Sgt. "Doc" Winters leads Miller's band across a New Haven park, possibly in a swinging rendition of a Sousa march which horrified traditionalists.

got him a leave and paid his way to Chicago so that he could sit in with the band at Christmas, traded nine other musicians to an Army outfit to get Trigger for his Air Forces Band, and without an instant's hesitation loaned Trigger $1,000 to buy a bass Trigger fancied.

When Mrs. Alpert was having their first child, Trigger missed a day's duty with the band to be with her. "The next day Glenn called me in. I explained that Connie had given birth to our first child. 'What's his name?' Glenn asked. I told him and all he said was, 'Dismissed.' Three hours later I got a $100 war bond made out to the baby."

In the spring of 1944, after a year of playing coast-to-coast recruiting broadcasts, Major Miller led overseas an expeditionary force of 20 strings, five trumpets, four trombones, a French horn, six reeds, two drummers, two pianists, two bassists, a guitarist, three arrangers, a copyist, five singers, two producers, an announcer, two administrators, two instrument repairmen and two executive producers.

None of this entourage was superfluous. Every man had a job and most were trained also to substitute for some other band member in an emergency. The band carried a vast supply of instrumental spare parts. When it finally reached Paris, many of these parts helped revive ailing horns among the less well-supplied U.S. Army Band. The band's director, Ray McKinley remembered, wept with gratitude.

Some sidemen remember how they hated Miller for bucking the brass until he got permission to drag the band out of London, where they wanted to go sight-seeing, to new barracks, with bomb shelters, in the town of Bedford. German rocket bombs were hitting London, and Miller felt his band was unsafe. A buzz bomb demolished the band's London barracks the day after they left them.

Major Miller to General Smith: No

Miller was never much daunted by brass, musical or military. Ray McKinley recalled that General Walter Bedell Smith, a tough infantryman who was then Eisenhower's Chief of Staff in Europe, once summoned Miller to Paris to offer him command of the U.S. Army Band. Miller said, "No, thank you, sir."

"And why not, Major?" asked "Beedle" Smith who seldom heard the word "no."

"I don't understand that kind of music, sir," said Miller.

"That's all, Major," said Bedell Smith. A little later he emerged from his office, asked his secretary for his ulcer pills and remarked, "That damn Miller—well, at least he knows what he wants."

He did, indeed—and also what he didn't want.

His various groups were enormously popular on their personal appearances and their broadcasts for the BBC, but *Metronome* did print one soldier's complaint that Sam Donahue's Navy band was putting out better jazz. Miller responded furiously that he was playing to please the majority of the troops. His temper, never very thick, was wearing thin at having been kept for so long so far away from the combat troops he wanted to entertain. He was anxious to leave for Paris to arrange for the band's appearance there.

On the foggy afternoon of Dec. 15, 1944, Miller and two others took off in a small plane for Paris. Nobody will ever know for sure why the normally cautious Miller did not wait for a better day or a bigger plane. Ten days later, on Christmas Day, the New York *Times* reported: "Major Glenn Miller, director of the United States Air Forces Band, is missing on a flight from England to Paris, it was announced today. No trace of the plane has been found." None ever was.

"Everybody had a sense of personal loss," Peanuts Hucko said. Miller left a hole where he had been. For many of his sidemen it was the end of a dream.

"After the war," Peanuts said, "he was going to take the guys he picked that wanted to go and start a new band. He would guarantee us $300 a week, work or no. Those that had families, he would guarantee their homes."

"I've bought some land in Santa Ana, California," Miller told Alpert, "and I'm going to build houses on this land and sell them to you guys that want them—family guys like you, Trigger—and the houses are going to be designed something like this." Alpert kept for years the sketch Miller drew of the house he would build for Trigger.

Trying to do it Glenn's way

Miller had worked out a scheme for basing and working mostly in California and working a few months of the year in New York and on the road. And he planned to improve his music, as he always had.

"He was moving toward a different sound," Peanuts said. "He would have been bigger than ever."

"He once said to me," Ray McKinley recalled, " 'I've gone as far as I can go with the saxophone sound. I've got to have something new.' He was going to keep this same band, maybe with a few less violins—he had about 20 or so—and he said, 'I'm going to get the best and the most beautiful girl singer in the world, and I'll have you and Tex.' And I said, 'How are you going to have me and Tex? We sing the same kinds of songs.' But he said, 'Don't worry, we'll work it out.' "

The war went on and so did the band, visiting 11 countries in 14 months and making 300 personal appearances. There was a feeling among the sidemen of "trying to do it like Glenn would've." Something of the same feeling seems to have inhibited arranger Jerry Gray who declined to take over the band after the war, saying, "I somehow didn't think it was right to step into Glenn's shoes then."

But the band did continue, first under Tex Beneke, then under Ray McKinley, and then under Buddy De Franco, with continued success.

"There's a story that he's still alive," Hal McIntyre once said, "in a sanatarium in California." Fans still write to Miller asking for autographed photographs, and occasionally somebody will step up to De Franco and say, "Hello, Mr. Miller, I haven't seen you for a long time."

And even for those who know he is dead, the Sound endures—haunting, evocative, the best-remembered music of the Era of Swing.

—GEORGE FRAZIER

The troopship *Santa Rosa* docks in New York in August 1945, crammed with returning GIs, including members of Glenn Miller's wartime band, celebrating the end of 14 months in Europe. Squeezed between trumpet and cymbals is one of the band's announcers, actor Broderick Crawford.

The Men Who Made the Music:
Harry James

Wide angle shot of a circus band of the 1920's. Zoom in to a small boy in an oversize bandsman's cap playing a snare drum with a crisp, professional beat. Come in tight, briefly, on the cap alone, then pull back to reveal, under the cap, the same boy, a few years older, now blowing a trumpet. Back off farther to show that he is now playing with a Salvation Army band. Cut to show a crowd of 1930s' swing fans pressing up to the bandstand, then pan back to the trumpeter, who is now wearing a wide-lapelled suit and a hairline mustache. As the trumpet continues to pour out a stream of incredibly high, rapid notes, cut to a crowd of middle-aged cruise passengers in black ties and formals dancing in a ship's ballroom. The trumpet continues playing as the camera backs steadily away to reveal, first, the trumpeter, heavier now and slightly graying, and then the whole ballroom, and finally cuts to a long shot of the ship sliding through moonlit Caribbean waters. With a final trumpet flourish, a title fills the screen: "The Harry James Story."

If such a movie is ever made, it probably won't tell the whole remarkable story of Harry Haag James, but it can hardly avoid presenting him as one of the few giants of the Swing Era who has bridged the generation gap and remained consistently popular without radically changing his style. He has developed a style compounded of his life and times. There are showbiz echoes in his trumpet—the get-'em-into-the-tent strains of a circus band. There is an element of the hot jazz he played with Benny Goodman, Ben Pollack, Lionel Hampton, Teddy Wilson and others among his peers. (Leopold Stokowski once listed Harry's *Strictly Instrumental* as one of his favorite jazz records.) And there is his dance music, sweet and swing, which he can pour into a classical mold like *Carnival of Venice* or into one of his originals like *Music Makers* or into the latest Beatles tune.

In addition to a remarkable general music adaptability, James is an instrumentalist of phenomenal power, range

and control. Christian Darnton, erudite author of *You And Music,* might have been thinking of James when he wrote: "Many of the feats of virtuosity executed by jazz players may smack of the vaudeville stunt. Nevertheless, the remarkable agility which first-class players show, as well as their ability to produce notes at the top extreme of the instruments' compasses, has set a wholesomely high standard for the orchestral player."

James has wisely never tried to be all things to all fans. One Louis Armstrong is probably enough for this world. Jimmy McPartland can sound so like the late Leon ("Bix") Beiderbecke, the great jazz trumpeter, that a few years ago a Chicagoan pausing outside the Brass Rail Theater Bar, where McPartland was playing, exclaimed, "My God, it's Bix!" But when Warner Brothers made *Young Man with a Horn,* from the 1938 novel whose protagonist is supposedly based on Bix, they hired James to play the trumpet solos mimed on the screen by Kirk Douglas.

The Warner Brothers executives were right. For most people who make no distinction among the various branches of jazz, Harry James is *the* archetypical hot trumpeter. If he has not created any musical institutions like the Glenn Miller Sound, he has proved himself one of the most imaginative of adapters and has remained one of the most sought-after and, to all appearances, best-adjusted musicians in modern history.

Too loud for Lawrence Welk

Harry James was born on March 15, 1916 in Albany, Ga., the only child of Everette Robert and Maybelle James. He was born in Albany because the Mighty Haag Circus, which featured his mother as an "iron jaw" aerialist and his father as band director, was playing there. They middle-named Harry in honor of the show.

Little Harry began his entertainment career at 5 as a contortionist. He now says that but for a mastoid operation, he might have wound up as the world's oldest living and still active human pretzel. As it was, he switched to playing drums and at 7 was good enough to substitute for the band's regular drummer. At 8 he began learning trumpet from his father and at 11 occupied a regular chair in the Christy Brothers Circus band.

In Beaumont, Texas, where the troupe wintered, Harry

A determined Harry James, 7, his career as a contortionist cut short by illness, begins a new life as substitute drummer in the Christy Brothers Circus band. He took to downbeats as easily as to back bends and at 8 began studying trumpet.

The Texas-based Doc Ross band of 1934 includes a young trumpeter who grins from a seat second from left in the rear row.

played the trumpet with a Salvation Army band, not out of religious zeal but, as he recalled, "just because I felt like playing and helping them out." When Harry was 14 his parents left the circus and settled in Beaumont. Soon after, Harry dropped out of school to earn his own living as a sideman in small-time Texas orchestras. One night, while still in short pants, Harry presented himself to Lawrence Welk, who was ah-one-, ah-twoing it on a Texas date. "You don't happen to be looking for a trumpet player, do you?" Harry asked. "I don't know, son," replied Welk. "I'd have to hear you play first." Harry blasted out a demonstration. "You play too loud for my band," Welk decided.

The kick Harry might have added to Welk's "Champagne Music" went instead to a series of regional orchestras—including those of Herman Waldman, a popular leader in the Southwest; Hogan Hancock and Ligon Smith, who operated out of Dallas and Fort Worth; and Joe Gill, whose Phillips Flyers worked out of St. Louis. While playing in Chicago with Art Hicks, Harry was picked up by Ben Pollack, the old jazz drummer who employed so many notable swing musicians.

Shorty Sherock, another Pollack trumpeter, roomed with Harry and remembered him later as a formidable technician. "He could play anything on the trumpet," Sherock said. "One time he walked into a room while a clarinet player was trying a difficult passage which he just couldn't seem to get. James said it would be nothing for him to play, even on the trumpet. Everybody scoffed at that, of course, and a lot of bets were made. Harry played the passage beautifully,

After leaving the Art Hicks band in 1936 to join Ben Pollack, James is photographed with fellow sidemen, trumpeter Shorty Sherock (left) and trombonist Bruce Squires.

picked up the money and left." While with Pollack, Harry also produced his first hint of larger musical abilities. He wrote a novelty number called *Peckin'*, which started a new national dance craze and launched Harry toward the top.

Among those who became aware of Harry was Benny Goodman's brother Irving. "Irving went to his brother," Harry recalled later, "and told him that he would quit his job—he was playing the trumpet with Benny—if Benny would hire me. So Goodman sent for me, and I went to New York." Benny Goodman later wrote that, after hearing Irving's recommendation, he turned on the radio to hear James. "I was keen to get him as soon as I could," Goodman remembered. The King of Swing wired his offer to Harry on Christmas Day 1936.

A *weird, wild rhythmic strain*

James quickly became a star in the Goodman constellation which then included such talented sidemen as Gene Krupa, Teddy Wilson and Ziggy Elman. The hot lead trumpet of the lanky kid from Texas beefed up B.G.'s brass section with some of the most crackling, hard-driving horn that the King's fans had ever heard. "The trumpet blasting of Harry James," marveled *Billboard*, "is musical violence personified." Singling out Harry's performance in Goodman's recording of *Sing, Sing, Sing,* Tom Collins of *Down Beat*

rhapsodized: "Picking up a weird, wild rhythmic strain, Harry James pilots his trumpet through some of the strangest improvising . . . that has ever 'attacked' your ears. It is barbaric in its figures and its attack."

Goodman has said that Harry "ranks with the best brass men in the country. [He has] a tremendous range and a wonderful bite in his playing. He always had fine ideas, and they kept improving all the time." Harry himself once described his style this way: "Personally, I like and play a rolling style in two- or four-bar phrases. To play this rolling style, or lots-of-notes style . . . you must have a basic knowledge of chords and progression [and] perfect control of your instrument." Of his technique, Harry added: "When you make a good, clean entrance and a 'planted' exit, your playing has acquired polish. It is only natural that a good beginning will enable you to create ideas more freely."

Harry spent on new horns some of the first money he earned from Goodman. He wanted to play his best when the band, then on the road, went to Hollywood to make the movie *Hollywood Hotel*. A bus was to deliver the band to Marshalltown, Iowa, where the Los Angeles Limited would make a special whistle stop to pick them up. The bus arrived with only minutes to spare.

"Harry James was the first one off," Benny Goodman recalled, "with his instrument case under his arm (he had

Making *Hollywood Hotel,* star Dick Powell gets a ride, James marches under a sign and Goodman sports a "bearskin" hat.

Unable to sit still, some jitterbugs dance onstage during James's engagement at New York's Paramount Theater in 1943.

lost a pet trumpet just as we started on the trip and was taking no chances . . .) when he suddenly remembered he had left his jacket on the bus. He put down the trumpet case (which was a double one, with two wonderful Selmer trumpets in it that he had picked up at the factory in Elkhart only a week or so before) and jumped back on the bus again. Just at this minute the station agent ran up and told the driver to pull out and drive down to the other end of the platform. . . . He put the car in reverse, and ran clean over Harry's two trumpets. There they were, flat as a sheet of music. Harry almost collapsed. . . ." The train arrived but failed to stop. The engineer had fallen asleep. Harry with his two flat trumpets got back on the bus with the other exhausted musicians for another long bus ride to catch the train at the next possible stop.

Among Harry's fervent admirers at that time was Louise Tobin, a baby-faced girl singer from Denton, Texas, who in private life was Mrs. Harry James. They had married in

their teens when Harry was playing with the Art Hicks band and she was a fledgling singer.

"Not long after I met him," Louise recalled later, "out of the blue, he said, 'Do you think you could love me?' I said, 'What's your name—Harry who?' I think what truly attracted him to me was that I was so unsophisticated and in awe of everything. He used to educate me in the swing language. He seemed very sophisticated to me. He knew the ropes. Later, after we were married and having our problems, I remember saying to Harry, 'You can't judge me because you brought me up.' "

They had two sons, neither of whom is close to Harry today. Few married musicians of the Swing Era had much time to get to know their families. Leaders were even busier than sidemen and Harry was determined to be a leader.

Like Glenn Miller and most other ambitious sidemen, James dreamed of forming his own band, and in January 1939, with $4,500 borrowed from Goodman in return for a one-third interest in the new enterprise, Harry organized his Music Makers. Like Harry's music, the band's uniforms had a touch of the circus—they wore red mess jackets, white bow ties and winged collars. The music was even louder than the clothes and people took notice. "Strictly for swing kicks," said *Metronome* in 1940, "Harry James has the greatest white band in the country."

Metronome was a little ahead of the public. The James band got enough engagements to keep going but was not making much money. Goodman sold his interest back to James for $19,500, according to James—a profit for Goodman of about $800 a month on his investment.

The honeyed touch of dainty strings

To meet the wartime demand for sweeter, more sentimental songs, Harry diluted his jazz-oriented jump with softer sounds. He began adding strings—first an experimental quartet, then more strings, until he finally had 24.

"I added strings," he said later, "because I always liked strings and it gave us more variety. Naturally I hoped the public would like it, but I played what I liked." He tempered his own trumpet, playing more wailing melodies and fewer torrid improvisations. Jazz purists were appalled by what they considered a segue into schmaltz. "It would be a shame to discover that the Harry James band had really lost [its] thrilling drive," said *Metronome*.

Yet Harry's new sentimental emphasis, initiated during the early days of World War II, touched more American heartstrings than his music ever had before. On May 20, 1941 Harry recorded (on the B side of a platter) an old Al Jolson favorite, *You Made Me Love You*, in which his trumpet, backed by his dainty strings, poured on the quavers like honey on hushpuppies. For two weeks disc jockey Martin Block gave the recording a big ride on his show, and crowds began to line up for Harry's personal appearances. *You Made Me Love You* became Harry's first big hit record

Comparatively restrained James fans applaud at Paramount. Some began lining up at 4 a.m., brought lunch and stayed all day.

James is a baseball nut. In his first year with Benny Goodman he was captain, pitcher and heaviest hitter of the band's undefeated team. He played hard; at left, he assumes a menacing stance at the plate and takes a mighty swipe at the ball. He once broke his right foot sliding into third and for some weeks had to perform seated, propped on suitcases (above).

Harry furnishes a hot obbligato as Nancy Walker belts

Harry and his second wife, movie star Betty Grable, fondly observe their daughter Vicki's early interest in music.

out *Alive and Kicking* in *Best Foot Forward*, one of Harry's movies. Film also features football parody *Buckle Down, Winsocki*.

and the song for which he is most remembered. He went up to the top of the charts with Miller, Goodman and Tommy Dorsey. In 1941 he placed second among soloists in *Down Beat's* annual poll, topped only by Benny Goodman.

The band was ably supported by Helen Forrest, a warm and tender vocalist who had sung with Shaw and Goodman, and Corky Corcoran, a big-toned tenor sax virtuoso whom Harry had not only hired but had adopted because Corcoran was only 17 and legally too young to work unless accompanied by a parent or a guardian. James went on to turn out an unforgettable series of wartime hits, like *I Cried for You, I Had the Craziest Dream, I've Heard That Song Before,* and *I'll Get By.* He never stopped playing swing, however, and in the spring of 1943 the band's performances in New York City's Paramount Theater drew such a mob of jitterbugs in zoot suits and bobby sox that police had to be called out to prevent a riot. *PM's* Max Lerner likened the scene to the ancient Greek revels of Dionysus—"only instead of the radiant young god you get a tallish young man with a horn."

"Each generation has to have its own craze and its own dance," Harry said of the jitterbugs, "and that's what it was then."

Another notable James vocalist had come to him by air in 1939. Harry and Louise were working in New York and finding the times far from easy. "Money was hard to come by then," Louise has recalled. The band was not doing well and Harry was looking for a boy singer. They were listening to the radio in their hotel room, Louise remembered. "Honey," she said suddenly, "listen to this boy sing." Harry listened and the next day went to an Englewood, N.J. road-house called the Rustic Cabin, where he signed up the youth, named Frank Sinatra, who had been singing at the Cabin for $25 a week and every day for nothing on three different New York radio stations.

Sinatra's success with James was modest. Their recording of *All or Nothing at All* sold a mere 8,000 copies—until 1943 when both men had arrived; then it perked up and eventually sold over a million. When Sinatra got a chance to join Tommy Dorsey, with five months still to run on his contract, James let him go—with no strings attached.

James replaced Sinatra with another unknown singer while auditioning some numbers for possible use by his band. "I don't like the tunes too much," James said, "but I sure like the way the kid sings." The kid, Dick Haymes, sang successfully with Harry and for years thereafter.

A .300 average for an audition

Harry played American Legion baseball in Beaumont as a youngster and was so promising a shortstop that he was once considered a prospect by the Detroit Tigers, who had a farm club in Beaumont. He organized his band into a team, complete with uniforms. "All the boys in Harry's band," said Louise Tobin, "were hired first because they could play baseball; second for their instruments." Musicians used to say you had to have a .300 batting average to get an audition with Harry.

"We carried more equipment for baseball than for music," recalled Frank Monte, Harry's longtime manager. "We'd be in that bus and we'd see something that could serve as a baseball field and, if we had an hour or so, we'd set up and play. In those days practically any bus you saw coming down the road was carrying another band, and we'd all stop and play baseball if we had the time. I'd always take our bus and stop at the first grocery store for beer, bologna and pickles, and we'd set up a picnic area too. That would save time. If we didn't have to stop and eat, we had more time to play baseball."

"Once we pulled off the road for a game," a former James sideman recalled, "and got stuck in a ditch and it cost Harry $300 to get towed out and we missed the date that night."

Harry gave baseball his all. He recorded a piece called *Dodger Fan Dance* in 1941 in honor of his favorite team, the Brooklyn Dodgers, and he once broke his right foot sliding into third and spent several weeks conducting from a chair.

Monopoly and Betty Grable, too

Harry also enjoyed Monopoly. "Harry always won," said Shorty Sherock, who played a lot of Monopoly with James when they were roommates. "He was a hell of a Monopoly player."

By 1943 Harry James was one of America's most successful bandleaders. He rounded out the American Dream on July 5 of that year, five days after his divorce from Louise Tobin, by marrying Betty Grable, pinup girl of a million GIs. "Harry never let me wear makeup—no lipstick," Louise said once. "Then he turned around and married a gorgeous showgirl."

Harry and Betty Grable had two daughters, and about this time he also took to buying and racing thoroughbreds. Some felt that Harry was neglecting his music, but his decision to disband the Music Makers in 1946 probably stemmed more from the general decline of big bands than from the pull of his outside interests. A few months later he bounced back with a new, streamlined outfit which, like his first band, had a string quartet and a lot of bounce. During the balance of the '40s, the vocalist-oriented '50s and the Rock Age '60s, Harry James, with only a few rests continued to lead a thriving orchestra which featured him in his old hits but also kept in tune with the times.

He was divorced from Betty Grable in 1965 and his 1967 marriage to Joan Boyd, a Las Vegas model, who bore him a son in 1968, also ended in divorce.

On a sunny winter day in 1970 he lunched contentedly with friends at a hotel near Miami. He was just back from playing for a swank Nassau cruise and was completing a hotel dance engagement before moving on to play at Las Vegas. The night before he had been beseiged by autograph-seeking admirers in the over-30 age bracket. "I don't make any concessions," he was saying, "but like anything else, there's good and bad rock and I play what I like, what I consider good." He was going on to say that he liked *Spinning Wheel* and *So Very Happy* when he had to break off. A pretty young thing in a miniskirt wanted her picture taken with him.

—BRUCE HENDERSON

At right, Harry rehearses for a 1968 Las Vegas reunion appearance with his 1939 "discovery," Francis Albert Sinatra.

The Music in This Volume

Glenn Miller's biggest hit, which sold millions of records, is based on a very old jazz riff, previously used in a Fletcher Henderson tune called *Hot and Anxious*. Artie Shaw used to play arranger Joe Garland's embellishment of the riff under the slightly cooler title of *In the Mood* but never recorded it because it ran some eight minutes. Miller, a gifted editor, pared it down to fit one side of a 78. "Glenn would get the scissors out and start editing," said Ray McKinley, a former Miller drummer and vocalist, remembering how Miller improved the work of his arrangers. "A cut here, a cut there, do this, do that, and he'd cut it down to the meat and potatoes of the tune and it would be a good arrangement." Like Miller's *Little Brown Jug*, *In the Mood* is notable for simplicity and strength. From the saxes playing in unison on the famous intro, to the tenor sax dialogue, to the protracted, suspense-building ending, it is a fine example of the addictive Miller Sound.

Both Al Jolson and Judy Garland achieved notable performances of this tearjerker. Harry James liked the way Judy sang it and echoed her style in an instrumental he made, without great expectations, for the B side of a 1941 record. Disc jockey Martin Block took a fancy to the side and played it repeatedly for two weeks on his "Make Believe Ballroom" radio show. "We arrived in New York for a booking at the Strand in Brooklyn," James said later, "and saw these huge crowds lined up around the theater. We thought it was a fire or something. I walked up to some people and asked them what was happening and they said they were there to hear Harry James play *You Made Me Love You*. I couldn't believe it." Harry's trumpet expertly combines sugar and spice as the tune pulses romantically to a soft, insistent cymbal beat. The string quartet Harry used experimentally in this one blended so well with the band that he later added still more strings, to the distress of some jazz fanciers.

In 1939 Artie Shaw was in Acapulco recuperating from agranulocytosis, a blood disease, escaping the bobby-soxers and thinking out his identity as a musician. "Acapulco wasn't like it is now," he says. "It was just a little fishing village then. A mariachi band used to play *Frenesi* all the time and I liked it. I thought it was a Mexican folk tune." Actually it was a new hit by Mexican composer-lyricist Alberto Dominguez. When Shaw returned to Hollywood he recorded it, using the string and woodwind treatment he called "the sound of a small symphony orchestra with a jazz band buried in it." Issued as the B side of *Adios, Mariquita Linda*, *Frenesi* was a fast-starting hit. *Down Beat* called the new band "a baby Kostelanetz outfit—with more guts" and said, "Artie the unpredictable remains so." The reviewer liked the solo clarinet's "spiraling around on arpeggios and technically brilliant passages which have always been peculiar to the Shavian style" and added: "Brilliant music, this, combining original orchestration with facile performance. But certainly not hot jazz as Artie has played in the past." Yet *Frenesi* generates its own kind of heat with a lovely blending of swing and strings, a light, firm beat and an appeal to the feet and to the emotions.

"We'd be on the road, we'd do the one-night stands," Les Brown recalled, "and then we'd like to 'sit down' for eight or ten weeks. That's what we were doing in the summer of '41 at the Log Cabin Farms in Armonk, New York. We were doing a lot of swinging the classics—*Marche Slàve*, the *Anvil Chorus*. I don't remember whether I thought of this or whether my arranger, Ben Homer, did." Whoever thought of it, Homer arranged the Farandole from Georges Bizet's *L'Arlésienne* music and called it "Bizet Had His Day." Because that sounded too negative they changed "had" to "has." Bizet continues to have his day in this one which has become a classic in its own right. "We still get requests for it," said Les, "for 'that Bizerte thing' or 'the Biz-ett piece.' We always know what they mean." It's the kind of tune people remember. The stompy rhythm, the hand-clapping, the united "Hey!" of the sidemen and some happy solos make Bizet's day a lot of fun.

"It was one of the very first full orchestrations I ever made," said the distinguished arranger Sy Oliver when asked about *Deep River* and the other Oliver-arranged numbers included in this volume. "I wrote it for Zack White in Cincinnati in 1928." Until then Sy had been writing only trumpet and sax choruses. He really spread his wings on this old spiritual, first published in a voice-and-piano arrangement by Henry Thacker Burleigh in 1917 but probably sung by slaves in other forms a century or more earlier. This arrangement, with its two-step approach and tricky sax chorus, has a 1928 sound. Tommy Dorsey recorded it, virtually unchanged, in 1941. It switches *Deep River* out of its usual dreamy, reverent channel and introduces some rapids and a cataract of drumming at the end. The band races downstream at a fast pace, with sensitive solos balancing driving drums, and makes port with a rousing three-chorus finale.

SIDE TWO

Band 1 TEMPTATION
Artie Shaw version

In 1940, about six months after he had naturalized Mexico's *Frenesi*, Artie Shaw recorded *Temptation*, a tune from the 1933 film *Going Hollywood*. It fitted the symphonic-style band he had in those days when he was talking about leading a 65-piece orchestra in a series of West Coast concerts of modern American music. It also had something of the Latin American pulse he was seeking. There was talk of his touring South America as featured clarinetist with Leopold Stokowski and he planned to do some recordings, he told a *Metronome* reporter, with "two Mexican tunes for every two American ones." The clean, clear tones of the clarinet in this arrangement contrast with the rather brooding atmosphere created by lavish use of strings and tom-toms.

Band 2 TUXEDO JUNCTION
Glenn Miller version

Erskine Hawkins recorded this first but Glenn Miller made it truly famous. As a student at Alabama State College, Hawkins played trumpet in a dance band along with Julian Dash and William Johnson. The three worked up a little tune from a musical phrase Dash had originated. After college, Dash joined the new Hawkins band which developed a "head" (unwritten) arrangement of the number. They used it first in Baltimore's Royal Theater when the management unexpectedly asked for an original number to accompany a vaudeville act. The audience liked it, so the band used it in Harlem's Savoy Ballroom as their sign-off piece, the number played at the end of each set. "Everybody inquired as to what we had played," said Dash, "so we developed it a little more."

For a recording date, Hawkins needed something for the B side of *Gin Mill Special*. "We'll put in the little number we play at the Savoy," said Hawkins. The "little number" had grown by then to a ten-minute performance and had to be cut drastically to fit one side of a 78. He called the tune *Tuxedo Junction* after a streetcar junction in the Tuxedo section of his native Birmingham.

Billy May, remembering many performances of the piece, recalled a "battle of the bands" at the Savoy between the Hawkins and Charlie Barnet bands: "When it came to *Tuxedo Junction*, everybody in the Barnet band knew the trumpet solo. All nine trumpets—four for Barnet, four for Hawkins and, of course, Erskine himself—played the same solo together. The place was packed and everybody just about flipped out."

Glenn Miller picked up the tune after it was published and, as Dash said, "The rest is history." Miller's recording was such a smash that he called his California ranch Tuxedo Junction. His version is slower than the Hawkins original, but its pervasive, almost hypnotic rhythm builds a suspense that demands the cathartic finale only a disciplined brass section can deliver.

Band 3 BLUES ON PARADE
Woody Herman version

"The Band That Plays The Blues" was a cooperative outfit launched in 1936. It was Woody Herman's first band and it played so many blues so often that during a gig in a Houston bistro it drew a peevish note from the manager: "You will kindly stop singing and playing those nigger blues." Fortunately for the archives of swing, Woody and the boys ignored him. Woody and Toby Tyler recast a Jiggs Noble arrangement called *Blues in Six Flats* to create *Blues on Parade*. It is one of the best of the early Herman blues, full of the excitement and drive that made his "Band That Plays The Blues"—and all subsequent Herman Herds—something special. In February 1940 *Down Beat* said: "Woody's get-off antics on alto are unlike anything he's waxed before; Steady Nelson's trumpeting, with that fine, round Texas tone, cuts through wonderfully." The review also noted a failing all too common to recordings of the period: "It doesn't do justice to the band as it sounds in person."

Band 4 CHEROKEE
Charlie Barnet version

Ray Noble, the elegant British bandleader who wrote things like *Goodnight Sweetheart* and *The Very Thought of You*, also composed an *Indian Suite* which included *Seminole*, *Comanche War Dance*, *Iroquois*—and *Cherokee*. The Noble pieces show few traces of North American Indian music, but *Cherokee*, at least, has done well among palefaces. At the Beverly Wilshire in Hollywood, Noble's music, according to *Billboard* of December 2, 1939, "brought Marlene Dietrich to a dance floor for the first time in Hollywood history," in the arms of James Stewart, her co-star in the film they were then making, *Destry Rides Again*. She requested *Cherokee* six times and next day had her secretary ask Noble for a recording of it. Count Basie and Charlie Barnet also recorded it. Billy May hurriedly wrote the gutty, hard-swinging Barnet arrangement in a car on the way to the recording studio. Charlie liked it so well that he dropped Vernon Duke's *New York Nocturne* as his signature tune and substituted *Cherokee*.

Band 5 BOOGIE WOOGIE ON ST. LOUIS BLUES
Earl Hines version

This vigorous version of the classic blues which W. C. Handy first published in 1914 leaped to life in 1940 on the stage of Chicago's Oriental Theater. A piano style called "boogie woogie," with eight beats to the bar in the left hand, was sweeping the country and the Hines band had been fooling around the night before with a boogie treatment of Handy's tune. The crowd loved what *Down Beat* later called its "subtle satire on boogie piano style" and the applause inspired George Dixon, straw boss of the band who also played trumpet and sax. "A thought came to mind to say something while Earl was playing," Dixon said, recalling the occasion. "Put out all the lights," he hollered like a man at a riotous rent party, "and call the law right now!" The audience laughed and when Hines started a solo, Dixon yelled, "Play till 1951!" Toward the end he shouted, "Don't quit now, Jack, don't quit now!" Hines left the hollers in when he made the record, which was the all-time "Fatha" Hines best seller. The sidemen, though subdued, are in there all the way, adding a touch of low register clarinet to the intro, putting saxes under Hines and letting the bass walk down at the end, but for most of the time Hines is in the foreground making the piano sound like a whole band.

SIDE THREE

Band 1 STEALIN' APPLES
Benny Goodman version

A toothbrush mustache, scholarly glasses and a downswept hairdo did little to disguise Benny Goodman as "Professor Magenbruch" in the 1948 movie *A Song Is Born*. The imposture would have failed anyway as soon as he started playing one of the numbers featured in the film, *Stealin' Apples*. This springy Fletcher Henderson arrangement shows instantly what made Benny King of Swing: the clean attacks and cutoffs, the phrasing, and the basically simple structure of Henderson's arrangement which, like all his arrangements for Benny, kept the focus on swing. The late Thomas ("Fats") Waller, that incredible fountain of music who was pianist, organist, composer, singer, comedian and occasional bandleader, wrote the tune. The lyrics were written by a frequent collaborator of Waller's, Andrea Razafinkeriefo, Duke of Antanariva and great-nephew of Ranavalona III, last Queen of Madagascar. This scion of Madagascan nobility, whose father died fighting the French conquerers of the island, was born in the U.S. and, as lyricist Andy Razaf, got his name on a good many records. The tune was a hit from its first performance on the July 8, 1939 "Camel Caravan" radio show. Its success was no surprise to Razaf. "It was the arrangement," he said. "Anything that Fletcher did caught on at once."

Band 2 STARDUST
Artie Shaw version

Hoagy Carmichael wrote *Stardust* in 1927 during a sentimental return to his alma mater, Indiana University. Bandleader Don Redman liked it and played it, but its popularity grew slowly. "It went from Don to Jean Goldkette," Carmichael says in his book, *Sometimes I Wonder,* "and then Isham Jones was handed a lead sheet that Victor Young mooched from Jean. It was the hard way in those days. Overnight hits on radio came later." Isham Jones's romantic rendering of *Stardust* inspired Mitchell Parish to write the beautiful lyrics. After that the song really took off, helped along by Walter Winchell's determined plugging of it. "In Italy it is called *Polvere di Stelle,*" said TIME in 1955, "and ranks with *O Sole Mio* as an all-time favorite. In Japan it is called *Sutaadasuto,* and is one number record stores are not afraid to overorder. In England, where pofessionals call it a 'gone evergreen,' no song has sold more copies. In the U.S. it is called *Stardust,* and is the nation's most durable hit—comfortable as an old shoe and yet rare as a glass slipper . . . a 20-year-old Indiana girl, mortally wounded in a shooting, asked to have *Stardust* played at her funeral." Besides Isham Jones, Tommy Dorsey, Benny Goodman and Glenn Miller all made fine recordings of *Stardust,* but none came close for tenderness, pathos, rapture and sheer beauty of sound to the version Lennie Hayton arranged for Shaw's big new band with string section. The ballad became one of the largest-selling instrumentals ever made. Shaw's *Stardust* is particularly memorable for its trumpet and trombone choruses and the lovely, dipping, soaring clarinet solo.

Band 3 LITTLE BROWN JUG
Glenn Miller version

J. E. Winner first published his words and music to *The Little Brown Jug* in 1869. Seventy years later Bill Finegan, one of the great arrangers of the Swing Era, expanded Winner's eight-bar jingle into a 16-chorus dance tune without spilling a drop. It was one of the first things Finegan did for Glenn Miller, who was himself a fine arranger with a talent for hiring other fine arrangers such as Finegan, Jerry Gray and Billy May. Miller's fruitful association with Finegan also produced numbers like *Hallelujah, Blue Skies* and *Runnin' Wild.*

In *Jug,* reviewers particularly liked the exciting tenor sax and trumpet solos. The band achieves a fine, relaxed but rocking beat, building momentum and volume gradually and neatly framing the solos. The tenor sax takes off like a relay runner, picking up the end of a trombone phrase. A later trombone solo is a tidy example of Miller's economical style. Canny use of cymbals throughout, plus artful shading and clever work with hat mutes in the brass section generate powerful swing. The Miller band used to get six requests a day for this one.

Band 4 WELL ALL RIGHT THEN
Jimmie Lunceford version

"It was a sign-off, a riff we played at the end of a set," said Sy Oliver. The musicians couldn't resist fooling around with these sign-off riffs, everybody pitched in new ideas and the riff outgrew its original purpose. "The trumpets would add a little and then the saxes and finally you'd have to change to something else for a sign-off," said Sy. On this one, a comical trombonist named Elmer Crumbley took to saying, "Well all right then!" at the end and Jimmie gave Crumbley's immortal line to the whole band (15 times plus one solo voice repetition at the end) when he recorded this head arrangement in 1939. Sy was playing trumpet in this session, his last recording with Lunceford before he moved on to another memorable career as an arranger with Tommy Dorsey. In this neat example of the easy, walking feeling the Lunceford band produced, the riff seems to grow just the way it originally did on the bandstand, with one improvisation sprouting from another and everybody eventually getting into the act.

Band 5 TWO O'CLOCK JUMP
Harry James version

Count Basie recorded his *One O'clock Jump* in 1937, Benny Goodman later added the number to his book, and one of his trumpeters, Harry James, began improvising on the trumpet solo, like a good jazzman. In his book, *The Kingdom of Swing,* Goodman recalls that ". . . we first started doing these descending trumpet runs in the last chorus of *One O'clock Jump* (so that everybody started referring to it as *Two O'clock Jump*) . . ." At that time it was more of a 1:30 jump, but when Harry recorded it with a studio group in 1938 before he had formed his own band, he still called it *One O'clock Jump.* In 1939 he recorded it again, this time going all the way and calling it *Two O'clock Jump.* It's still basically Basie with a little extra melody at the beginning and the descending trumpet runs Goodman mentions added at the end, but Harry's version gives it a new frenzy with the trumpet taking the chromatic scales oftener and more savagely. The boogie-woogie piano, with its "walking" left hand, is still there along with the familiar original Basie riff and the rising trombone glissandos. Whatever the hour, it jumps.

SIDE FOUR
Band 1 SUNRISE SERENADE
Glenn Miller version

"Frankie Carle wrote it and should have had the big success with it," said Ray McKinley, Miller's drummer, vocalist and eventual successor as bandleader, "but Glenn did." Miller had a way of picking up other people's tunes, like this one, which later became Carle's theme, and running to the top of the sales charts with them. He recorded *Sunrise Serenade* in 1939, the year he suddenly appeared in second place in both sweet and swing categories in the annual polls of both *Down Beat* and *Metronome.* He was now a formidable rival for Tommy Dorsey and for Benny Goodman, the respective first-place winners in sweet and swing. Miller's *Sunrise Serenade* stayed at or near the top of the best sellers week after week and competed hotly with Glen Gray's version for the nickels of juke box customers. It even did a smashing sheet music business which surprised *Billboard* because of "its difficult melody for homespun piano playing and vocalizing." Certainly the simple way Miller played it attracted customers. His blues-tinged arrangement, somewhat more robust than the Gray version, opens with clarinet and tenor sax taking the lead together (a Miller trademark), proceeds with a gently insistent theme, adds a poignant tenor solo and ends with the brass section hailing the sunrise.

Band 2 REDSKIN RHUMBA
Charlie Barnet version

"We just ran out of music," said Charlie Barnet, recalling the genesis of *Redskin Rhumba,* a classic example of an instant head arrangement. One night Barnet's orchestra was broadcasting live from the Lincoln Hotel in New York. The band was playing its closing number, *Cherokee,* when Charlie realized that if they stuck to their usual arrangement they would finish with several minutes to spare, leaving radio listeners with dead air or a frantically ad-libbing announcer. The band played on, improvising variations on *Cherokee.* "We stretched it and stretched it," said Barnet. The entertainment gap was successfully bridged and later Charlie wrote down a more fully developed version of the stretch-out. "When nobody writes down a head arrangement," he explained, "if somebody leaves, part of your arrangement has just walked off." During a period when the band could not use *Cherokee* as a theme because of a legal dispute, *Rhumba* was a useful substitute—and a flexible one: like work, as described in Parkinson's Law, it could be extended to fill the time available. The performance is a roaring, crackling romp with little rhumba feeling in it beyond the title but with plenty of growl trumpet, and a salty, jumping tenor solo set against a continuous repetition of wah-wahing trombones.

Bands 3 LONESOME ROAD Parts I and II
and 4 *Tommy Dorsey version*

Those diligent songsmiths Nat Shilkret and Gene Austin copyrighted in 1927 this familiar version of *Lonesome Road,* which is patterned on a traditional Negro work song. *Lonesome Road* was a feature of *The Show Boat,* a movie made so close to the dawn of the talkies that it was shot as a silent film and had a musical prologue added later. "I suppose I chose it because it was a nice, simple tune," said Bill Finegan, recalling his 1938 arrangement, "one of those pop, pseudo-folk-tunes. Most people think it's a spiritual. I thought so myself at the time. It was the first arrangement I ever did for Tommy Dorsey." Dorsey liked the arrangement so much that he recorded it on two sides of a 78, a rare extravagance in those days. Since Dorsey was already employing several arrangers, he couldn't offer Finegan a job. But one day Glenn Miller dropped

in, Tommy played *Lonesome Road* for him and Miller hired Finegan. The arrangement has some resemblances to Sy Oliver's arrangement of *Swanee River* in its simplicity and in the straightforward, pure-toned trombone solo. Finegan (who later was Oliver's fellow arranger in a U.S. Army band) may have been, at this early period, somewhat influenced by Oliver, but his subsequent career is proof of a great and original talent.

Band 4 CIRIBIRIBIN
**   *Harry James version***

Alberto Pestalozza (1851-1934) was an otherwise obscure Italian composer who in 1909 wrote a tune dripping with mandolin-saturated sentimentality which became so widely popular after Enrico Caruso sang it that most people, including Harry James, thought of it as a folk melody. Poor Pestalozza barely gets credit on rcord labels. James revised the tune in collaboration with Jack Lawrence and first performed it while still playing with Benny Goodman's band at the Paramount Theater. Benny's other dazzling trumpeter, Ziggy Elman, was making a big solo splash with *And the Angels Sing.* Harry, as he has since recalled, felt he needed an equally flashy solo. He liked to spur old warhorses (as he later did with *Flight of the Bumble-Bee* and *A Carnival in Venice*) so he chose *Ciribiribin.* Many singers, including Bing Crosby and the Andrews Sisters, followed the same urge, as did Frank Sinatra in an early recording with the James Band. But it was the later James instrumental version, and especially Harry's brilliant trumpeting, that really put Pestalozza over. After a deceptively sweet and heavy opening, the trumpet rips into exciting cadenzas, mounts the breaks in fast triplets and swings into the final ride-out.

SIDE FIVE
Band 1   SWANEE RIVER
**   *Tommy Dorsey version***

Stephen Foster called it *Old Folks at Home* when he published it in 1851 but everybody now calls the lovely melody "Swanee River." A white man, drawn toward but not really into the songs of a captive black people, wrote it. A black man, Sy Oliver, who was a Foster fan ("It wasn't corn when he wrote it, you know") with an expert ear for any kind of music, arranged it for a black band, Jimmie Lunceford's. "The band never played it well," said Oliver, thinking back, "and the Lunceford record didn't sell." Some five years later Oliver took the arrangement to Tommy Dorsey. "Dorsey did an excellent job on it and the record was a big success," Sy said. "It was the same arrangement. You know, I never thought about that white-black-white business before, but now that I think of it, Foster had finally come full cycle." Oliver's arrangement retains all of Foster's poignancy. The solos, especially the trombone, are framed with Oliver's pre-eminent skill. It is, as Oliver said, "an exercise in simplicity bearing out Foster's original feeling."

Band 2   MUSIC MAKERS
**   *Harry James version***

"The band was known as 'Harry James and His Music Makers,' " said Frank Monte, "but the tune wasn't popular until after *You Made Me Love You* became such a smash hit. After that, everything was popular, including *Music Makers.*" The tune is one of the few Harry wrote himself and this setting is by Jack Mathias, his staff arranger. A *Metronome* reviewer called this and other Mathias arrangements "interesting without ever getting too involved." One interesting aspect of this trumpet-player's tune is that it emphasizes the trumpet section rather than solo trumpet, and features a catchy riff melody, smooth-blending, gutty saxes and a seductive beat. Not everybody has always dug *Music Makers.* Glenn Miller once asked Billy May to arrange it for the Miller band. May took a dislike to the tune and deliberately prepared so bad an arrangement that the band never played it. In conducting the arrangement in this

volume, however, May obviously has laid aside his old reservations. *Music Makers* has stayed popular with most listeners. "It gets played every night," said Monte.

Band 3   LET'S DANCE
**   *Benny Goodman version***

What may be the world's most famous theme song first got on the air by a narrow margin. As Goodman says in his book, *The Kingdom of Swing,* "toward the end of September 1934, the word got around that the National Biscuit Company was planning to put on a big program at NBC . . . The setup called for a rhumba band, a sweet orchestra and a hot band. We had some idea we were being considered for the spot as the hot band." Representatives of the sponsor came to hear Goodman at the Music Hall. The band played all its best arrangements. "I, for one, really played as if my life depended on it, for, in a way, it did," says Goodman. They got the job, but, he says, "I later discovered that the sponsors had brought a group of employees up from their office, and asked them to vote for the band they liked best. We made it by one vote." The three-hour show, the longest sponsored program that had ever been broadcast, ran on 53 stations from December 1934 to May 1935. Each of the three bands opened its segment with *Let's Dance,* a tune arranged by George Bassman, which takes off from a swatch of *Invitation to the Dance* by the great German romantic composer, Carl Maria von Weber. The urgent beat, the fine alto solo, the jabbing brass in the last chorus and above all the lilting, lifting clarinet made this the theme song of an era.

Band 4   POMPTON TURNPIKE
**   *Charlie Barnet version***

On the Newark-Pompton Turnpike stands the Meadowbrook, one of the great dance halls of the Swing Era. Charlie Barnet often played here, and he gave the road's name to a tune which singer Dick Rogers and bandleader Will Osborne wrote and Billy May arranged for a 1940 record date. The number has a slow, swinging beat with a soprano sax providing excitement, but *Turnpike*'s most famous landmark is a lively dialogue with a muted trumpet mockingly echoing the brief sax phrases. *Met-*

ronome critic Gordon Wright commented: *"Pompton Turnpike* is a really solid bit, with an unnecessary Alphonse and Gaston act between Charlie and trumpeter Billy May." Charlie Barnet, recalling how sick he and the band got of playing the much-requested number, agreed. "It's trite," he said, "and doesn't leave much room for inventiveness." But to most listeners the duet still sounds gay and funny. Part of May's arrangement never made it onto wax. The juke boxes of 1940 could not adequately reproduce his brass ending, so Victor simply cut the finale in all its recordings of the tune. To please the fans, bands always tried to play their big numbers the way they had on the record and *Pompton Turnpike* when played live now always ends a few bars short, as it does in this performance.

Band 5   720 IN THE BOOKS
Jan Savitt version

Russian-born Jan Savitt, son of a drummer in an imperial regimental band, came to America in 1914. At 14 he was a violinist in the Philadelphia Symphony, where he rose to become Stokowski's concert master, and later studied with conductors Artur Rodzinski and Fritz Reiner. Savitt even organized his own string quartet before turning from the classics to form the Top Hatters, the first radio station house band to emerge as a real name band. It was one of the better groups of the Swing Era, noted for its shuffle rhythm, a propulsive beat built around a piano playing at double time. In 1939 Savitt and arranger Johnny Watson came up with a neat new number which had nice drive from a repeated and skillfully varied phrase along with some good trumpet, trombone and clarinet solos. It had everything but a name. All it had was its number, 720, in the band's library. In broadcasts from New York's Hotel Lincoln, Savitt appealed to his listeners for an appropriate title, but nobody seemed to have any inspired ideas so the riff tune remained just "720 in the books." Later Harold Adamson added lyrics, and Savitt's sensitive vocalist Bon Bon, one of the first black musicians to work regularly with a white band, made *720 in the Books* an even bigger hit.

SIDE SIX
Band 1   TAKE THE "A" TRAIN
Duke Ellington version

Composer-arranger Billy Strayhorn joined the Duke Ellington band in 1939 and "from that day forward," as jazz critic and historian Martin Williams says, "perhaps we shall never know who contributed what to the Ellington book." The tiny, modest, bespectacled Strayhorn became a kind of musical alter ego for Ellington, sometimes sitting in for him at the piano. In one of the first numbers he wrote for the Duke, Strayhorn produced *Take the "A" Train*, which became the band's signature. He got the title from the fact that when New York added to its other uptown subway routes the "D" train, which branched off to the Bronx, it was no longer a simple matter of taking any uptown train to get to Harlem. Strayhorn now had to remember to take the one marked "A."

His musical memo to himself is essentially a smooth and happy ride rocking along over velvety saxes with muted trumpet in the background. Brass increases the propulsive feeling and, at the end, the number trails quietly out of hearing like red taillights vanishing in a tunnel. The *"A" Train* made its slowest and saddest run in May 1967 at Strayhorn's funeral in St. Peter's Lutheran Church, New York City. Retired baseball star Jackie Robinson was one of the mourners who heard violinist Ray Nance and the Billy Taylor Trio open a collection of Strayhorn compositions with a dirgelike version of *"A" Train*. "I don't think there was a dry eye in the church," said Robinson.

Band 2   SNOWFALL
Claude Thornhill version

The late Claude Thornhill's mind was in Cuba when he wrote *Snowfall*. "It was originally part of a suite Claude wrote in the '30s and was called *Fountain in Havana*," said Bill Borden, a Thornhill authority, recalling the days when he was arranger for Thornhill's brand-new band. "When we brought the band into Balboa, California, in 1940 we had to have a theme and we picked that. We couldn't call it *Fountain in Havana*—though relations with Havana were better then than they are now. We thought of everything—'Waterfall,' everything—and finally picked this title." This arrangement was the first version of the Thornhill theme song. Claude also made a more complicated arrangement using the French horns he brought into the band after World War II. The echoing chords and lacy piano at the outset of this gentle, wistful tune display the softer side of swing. There is also a swell of ensemble sound typical of the band's fine use of dynamics. Thornhill liked to set up a soft, mellow mood with one of his one-finger piano solos, or through six delicately blown unison clarinets, and then suddenly throw in a burst of gorgeous ensemble sound.

In 1942 Thornhill was sent to Pearl Harbor with Artie Shaw's Navy band. He arrived just after the base Christmas party and was among those picked for the clean-up detail. To ease the chore, some USO girls started playing phonograph records, beginning with *Snowfall*. And there was Claude, pushing his broom.

Band 3   MOONLIGHT SERENADE
Glenn Miller version

Moonlight Serenade grew out of an arrangement Glenn Miller wrote as an assignment while studying for a time with the distinguished music theorist Joseph Schillinger. The piece was originally called "Now I Lay Me Down To Weep" with lyrics by Eddie Heyman, who also wrote the words to *Body and Soul*. Miller never recorded this version, but later, after Mitchell Parish had supplied new lyrics and a less tearful title, it became Glenn's theme song. It was immensely popular and millions of radio listeners found it maddening to have the tune cut off part way as it usually was when Miller broadcast from Glen Island Casino or Frank Dailey's Meadowbrook or the Cafe Rouge of the Hotel Pennsylvania. It is a serenely beautiful piece with a recurrent theme, rumbles of brass and nimble clarinet solos. Ray McKinley, recalling the days after the war when he led a re-formed Glenn Miller Band, said, "I've seen people stand up in front of the band and actually cry. You could almost forget about playing any new tunes. If you didn't play *Little Brown Jug, Tuxedo Junction, In The Mood, Moonlight Serenade* and so on, these people would take you outside and beat you up."

Bands 4   ANVIL CHORUS   Parts I and II
and 5   *Glenn Miller version*

"When Glenn asked me to do it," said Jerry Gray, recalling how he arranged this familiar bit of Verdi's *Il Trovatore* for Miller, "I was madder than hell. I said, 'What the hell can I do with a song like that?' But it became a challenge to me, so I sat down one hot summer night in Chicago and did a block arrangement. The band was enthusiastic. It was a bit of a back-breaker for the brass, but they liked it." So did Miller who recorded it on two sides of a 78, and often used it as a rousing finale for his radio broadcasts. The band gives it an operatic opening, tosses a bow in the direction of Verdi's melody and takes off on a well-hammered series of variations which build beautifully to a climax.

—PHILIP W. PAYNE

The Musicians Who Made the Recordings in This Volume

IN THE MOOD
LEADER: Glen Gray TRUMPETS: Manny Klein, Conrad Gozzo, Shorty Sherock, Pete Candoli, Cappy Lewis TROMBONES: Si Zentner, Murray McEachern, Joe Howard, Milt Bernhart, Tommy Pederson SAXOPHONES: Skeets Herfurt, Gus Bivona, Babe Russin, Plas Johnson, Chuck Gentry, Julie Jacob PIANO: Ray Sherman GUITAR: Jack Marshall BASS: Mike Rubin DRUMS: Nick Fatool

YOU MADE ME LOVE YOU
LEADER: Billy May TRUMPETS: James Zito, Shorty Sherock, Ray Triscari, Joe Graves, Uan Rasey TROMBONES: Lew McCreary, Milt Bernhart, Joe Howard, Ed Kusby SAXOPHONES: Jack Nimitz, Skeets Herfurt, Abe Most, Plas Johnson, Justin Gordon, Chuck Gentry VIOLINS: Darrel Terwilliger, John De Voogdt, James Getzoff, Sidney Sharp, Harry Bluestone, Gerald Vinci, Emil Briano, Paul Shure, Edward Bergman VIOLAS: Samuel Boghossian, Gareth Nuttycombe CELLOS: Raphael Kramer, Anne Goodman PIANO: Ray Sherman GUITAR: Jack Marshall BASS: Clifford Hils DRUMS: Nick Fatool

FRENESI
Same as YOU MADE ME LOVE YOU with Vincent de Rosa added on French horn, Gene Cipriano added on oboe, Skeets Herfurt and Justin Gordon also on flute, Chuck Gentry also on bass clarinet.

BIZET HAS HIS DAY
LEADER: Billy May TRUMPETS: James Zito, Shorty Sherock, John Audino, Joe Graves, Uan Rasey TROMBONES: Lew McCreary, Milt Bernhart, Joe Howard, Ed Kusby SAXOPHONES: Skeets Herfurt, Abe Most, Plas Johnson, Justin Gordon, Jack Nimitz PIANO: Ray Sherman GUITAR: Jack Marshall BASS: Rolly Bundock DRUMS: Nick Fatool

DEEP RIVER
LEADER: Billy May TRUMPETS: Pete Candoli, Shorty Sherock, John Audino, Joe Graves, Uan Rasey TROMBONES: Lew McCreary, Hoyt Bohannon, Joe Howard, Ed Kusby SAXOPHONES: Skeets Herfurt, Abe Most, Plas Johnson, Justin Gordon, Chuck Gentry PIANO: Ray Sherman GUITAR: Jack Marshall BASS: Clifford Hils DRUMS: Nick Fatool

TEMPTATION
Same as YOU MADE ME LOVE YOU

TUXEDO JUNCTION
LEADER: Billy May TRUMPETS: Pete Candoli, Shorty Sherock, Ray Triscari, Joe Graves, Uan Rasey TROMBONES: Lew McCreary, Hoyt Bohannon, Joe Howard, Ed Kusby SAXOPHONES: Skeets Herfurt, Abe Most, Plas Johnson, Justin Gordon, Chuck Gentry PIANO: Ray Sherman GUITAR: Jack Marshall BASS: Rolly Bundock DRUMS: Nick Fatool

BLUES ON PARADE
Same as IN THE MOOD

CHEROKEE
LEADER: Glen Gray TRUMPETS: Manny Klein, Conrad Gozzo, Shorty Sherock, Pete Candoli TROMBONES: Si Zentner, Murray McEachern, Joe Howard, Benny Benson SAXOPHONES: Skeets Herfurt, Gus Bivona, Babe Russin, Julie Jacob, Chuck Gentry PIANO: Ray Sherman GUITAR: Jack Marshall BASS: Mike Rubin DRUMS: Nick Fatool

BOOGIE WOOGIE ON ST. LOUIS BLUES
Same as CHEROKEE

STEALIN' APPLES
Same as BIZET HAS HIS DAY

STARDUST
Same as YOU MADE ME LOVE YOU

LITTLE BROWN JUG
Same as TUXEDO JUNCTION

WELL ALL RIGHT THEN
LEADER: Billy May TRUMPETS: Conrad Gozzo, Manny Klein, Ollie Mitchell, Pete Candoli, Vito Mangano TROMBONES: Trummy Young, Ed Kusby, Si Zentner, Dick Noel, Joe Howard SAXOPHONES: Willie Smith, Joe Thomas, Willie Schwartz, Ted Nash, Chuck Gentry, Bob Lawson PIANO: Jimmy Rowles GUITAR: Al Hendrickson BASS: Joe Mondragon DRUMS: Alvin Stoller

TWO O'CLOCK JUMP
Same as BIZET HAS HIS DAY

SUNRISE SERENADE
Same as TUXEDO JUNCTION

REDSKIN RHUMBA
LEADER: Glen Gray TRUMPETS: Conrad Gozzo, Shorty Sherock, Joe Graves, Uan Rasey TROMBONES: Joe Howard, Ed Kusby, Milt Bernhart, Lew McCreary SAXOPHONES: Abe Most, Skeets Herfurt, Babe Russin, Plas Johnson, Chuck Gentry PIANO: Ray Sherman GUITAR: Jack Marshall BASS: Mike Rubin DRUMS: Nick Fatool

LONESOME ROAD
Same as DEEP RIVER

CIRIBIRIBIN
Same as REDSKIN RHUMBA

SWANEE RIVER
Same as DEEP RIVER

MUSIC MAKERS
Same as BIZET HAS HIS DAY

LET'S DANCE
Same as REDSKIN RHUMBA

POMPTON TURNPIKE
Same as DEEP RIVER

720 IN THE BOOKS
Same as CHEROKEE

TAKE THE "A" TRAIN
Same as CHEROKEE

SNOWFALL
Same as CHEROKEE

MOONLIGHT SERENADE
Same as REDSKIN RHUMBA

ANVIL CHORUS
Same as TUXEDO JUNCTION

Discography
The original recordings of the
selections re-created in this volume

IN THE MOOD
Composer and arranger: Joseph C. Garland.
Recorded for Bluebird July 26, August 1, 1939

TRUMPETS	SAXOPHONES
Clyde Hurley	Hal McIntyre
Mickey McMickle	Tex Beneke
Leigh Knowles	°Willie Schwartz
TROMBONES	PIANO
Glenn Miller	Chummy MacGregor
Al Mastren	GUITAR
Paul Tanner	Richard Fisher
DRUMS	BASS
Maurice Purtill	°Rolly Bundock

YOU MADE ME LOVE YOU
Composer: James V. Monaco. Arranger:
Harry James. Recorded for Columbia
May 20, 1941

TRUMPETS	VIOLINS
Harry James	Glenn Herzer
Claude Bowen	Leo Zorn
Al Stearns	Sam Rosenblum
TROMBONES	Alex Pevsner
Dalton Rizzotto	CELLO
°Hoyt Bohannon	Al Friede
Harry Rodgers	PIANO
SAXOPHONES	Al Lerner
Vido Musso	GUITAR
Claude Lakey	Ben Heller
Sam Marowitz	BASS
°Chuck Gentry	Thurman Teague
DRUMS	
Mickey Scrima	

FRENESI
Composer: Alberto Dominguez. Arrangers:
Artie Shaw and William Grant Still.
Recorded for Victor March 3, 1940

TRUMPETS	VIOLINS
Charlie Margulies	Mark Levant
°Manny Klein	°Harry Bluestone
George Thow	Peter Eisenberg
TROMBONES	Robert Barene
Randall Miller	Sid Brokaw
Bill Rank	Dave Cracov
Babe Bowman	Alex Law
CLARINET	Jerry Joyce
Artie Shaw	VIOLAS
SAXOPHONES	David Sturkin
Blake Reynolds	Stanley Spiegelman
Bud Carlton	Jack Gray
Dick Clark	CELLOS
Jack Stacey	Irving Lipschultz
PIANO	Jules Tannenbaum
Stan Wrightsman	FLUTE
GUITAR	Morton Ruderman
Bobby Sherwood	OBOE
BASS	Phil Memoli
Jud DeNaut	BASS CLARINET
DRUMS	Joe Krechter
Carl Maus	FRENCH HORN
	Jack Cave

BIZET HAS HIS DAY
Composer: Georges Bizet. Arranger: Ben
Homer. Recorded for Okeh September 17,
1941

TRUMPETS	SAXOPHONES
Bob Thorne	Les Brown
Eddie Bailey	Steve Madrick
Don Jacoby	°Abe Most
TROMBONES	Wolffe Tayne
°Si Zentner	Eddie Scheer
Warren Brown	PIANO
Ronnie Chase	Billy Rowland
GUITAR	BASS
Joe Petroni	John Knepper
DRUMS	
Nat Polen	

DEEP RIVER
Traditional. Arranger: Sy Oliver.
Recorded for Victor February 17, 1941

TRUMPETS	SAXOPHONES
Ziggy Elman	Fred Stulce
Ray Linn	Johnny Mince
Chuck Peterson	Paul Mason
Jimmy Blake	Heinie Beau
TROMBONES	Don Lodice
Tommy Dorsey	PIANO
Les Jenkins	Joe Bushkin
George Arus	GUITAR
Lowell Martin	Clark Yocum
DRUMS	BASS
Buddy Rich	Sid Weiss

TEMPTATION
Composer: Nacio Herb Brown. Arranger:
Lennie Hayton. Recorded for Victor
September 7, 1940

TRUMPETS	CLARINET
George Wendt	Artie Shaw
Jimmy Cathcart	VIOLINS
Billy Butterfield	T. Boardman
TROMBONES	Ted Klages
Jack Jenney	Bob Bower
Vernon Brown	B. Morrow
SAXOPHONES	Al Beller
Les Robinson	Eugene Lamas
Neely Plumb	VIOLAS
Bus Bassey	Allan Harshman
Jerry Jerome	Kenneth Collins
BASS	CELLO
Jud DeNaut	Fred Goerner
DRUMS	PIANO
°Nick Fatool	Johnny Guarnieri
	GUITAR
	°Al Hendrickson

TUXEDO JUNCTION
Composers: Erskine Hawkins, Julian Dash
and William Johnson. "Head" arrangement,
based on William Johnson's arrangement for
the Erskine Hawkins band. Recorded for
Bluebird February 5, 1940

TRUMPETS	SAXOPHONES
Clyde Hurley	Hal McIntyre
Mickey McMickle	Tex Beneke
Leigh Knowles	°Willie Schwartz
Johnny Best	Jimmy Abato
TROMBONES	Al Klink
Glenn Miller	PIANO
Tommy Mack	Chummy MacGregor
Paul Tanner	GUITAR
Frank D'Annolfo	Richard Fisher
DRUMS	BASS
Maurice Purtill	°Rolly Bundock

BLUES ON PARADE
Composers: Toby Tyler and Woody Herman.
Arranger: Jiggs Noble. Recorded for Decca
December 13, 1939

TRUMPETS	CLARINET
°Cappy Lewis	Woody Herman
Steady Nelson	SAXOPHONES
Bob Price	Joe Denton
FLUGELHORN	Ray Hopfner
Joe Bishop	Saxie Mansfield
TROMBONES	Ronnie Perry
Neal Reid	VIOLIN
Toby Tyler	Nick Hupfer
BASS	PIANO
Walt Yoder	Tommy Linehan
DRUMS	GUITAR
Frank Carlson	Hy White

CHEROKEE
Composer: Ray Noble. Arranger: °Billy
May. Recorded for Bluebird July 17, 1939

TRUMPETS	SAXOPHONES
Bobby Burnet	Charlie Barnet
Johnny Owens	Kurt Bloom
°Billy May	Gene Kinsey
TROMBONES	Don McCook
Ben Hall	Jimmy Lamare
Don Ruppersberg	PIANO
Bill Robertson	Bill Miller
GUITAR	BASS
Bus Etri	Phil Stephens
DRUMS	
Ray Michaels	

BOOGIE WOOGIE ON ST. LOUIS BLUES
Composer: W. C. Handy. "Head"
arrangement. Recorded for Bluebird
February 13, 1940

TRUMPETS	SAXOPHONES
Walter Fuller	James Mundy
Milton Fletcher	Robert Crowder
Edward Simms	Omer Simeon
	LeRoy Harris

°Took part in one or more of the re-creations in this volume.

TRUMPET & SAXOPHONE	PIANO
George Dixon	Earl Hines
TROMBONES	GUITAR
Eddie Burke	Claude Roberts
John Ewing	BASS
Joe McLewis	Quinn Wilson
	DRUMS
	Alvin Burroughs

STEALIN' APPLES
Composer: Thomas "Fats" Waller. Arranger: Fletcher Henderson. Recorded for Columbia August 11, 1939

TRUMPETS	CLARINET
Ziggy Elman	Benny Goodman
Chris Griffin	SAXOPHONES
Corky Cornelius	Toots Mondello
TROMBONES	Buff Estes
Vernon Brown	Bus Bassey
Red Ballard	Jerry Jerome
Bruce Squires	PIANO
BASS	Fletcher Henderson
Artie Bernstein	GUITAR
DRUMS	Arnold Covarrubias
°Nick Fatool	

STARDUST
Composer: Hoagy Carmichael. Arrangers: Artie Shaw and Lennie Hayton. Recorded for Victor October 7, 1940

TRUMPETS	CLARINET
George Wendt	Artie Shaw
Jimmy Cathcart	VIOLINS
Billy Butterfield	T. Boardman
TROMBONES	Ted Klages
Jack Jenney	Bob Bower
Vernon Brown	B. Morrow
SAXOPHONES	Al Beller
Artie Shaw	Eugene Lamas
Les Robinson	VIOLAS
Neely Plumb	Allan Harshman
Bus Bassey	Kenneth Collins
Jerry Jerome	CELLO
BASS	Fred Goerner
Jud DeNaut	PIANO
DRUMS	Johnny Guarnieri
°Nick Fatool	GUITAR
	°Al Hendrickson

LITTLE BROWN JUG
Composer: J. E. Winner. Arranger: Bill Finegan. Recorded for Bluebird April 10, 1939

TRUMPETS	SAXOPHONES
Bob Price	Hal McIntyre
Mickey McMickle	Tex Beneke
Leigh Knowles	°Willie Schwartz
TROMBONES	Stanley Aronson
Glenn Miller	Al Klink
Al Mastren	PIANO
Paul Tanner	Chummy MacGregor
BASS	GUITAR
°Rolly Bundock	Allan Reuss
DRUMS	
Maurice Purtill	

WELL, ALL RIGHT THEN
"Head" arrangement by the Jimmie Lunceford band. Recorded for Vocalion May 17, 1939

TRUMPETS	SAXOPHONES
Eddie Tompkins	°Willie Smith
Paul Webster	Earl Carruthers
Sy Oliver	Ted Buckner
TROMBONES	°Joe Thomas
°Trummy Young	Dan Grissom
Elmer Crumbley	PIANO
Russell Bowles	Edwin Wilcox
BASS	GUITAR
Moses Allen	Al Norris
DRUMS	
James Crawford	

TWO O'CLOCK JUMP
Composers: Count Basie, Benny Goodman, Harry James. Arrangers: Count Basie and Harry James. Recorded for Brunswick February 20, 1939

TRUMPETS	SAXOPHONES
Harry James	Dave Matthews
Tommy Gonsoulin	Claude Lakey
Claude Bowen	Bill Luther
Jack Palmer	Drew Page
TROMBONES	PIANO
Russell Brown	Jack Gardner
Truett Jones	GUITAR
DRUMS	Bryan Kent
Ralph Hawkins	BASS
	Thurman Teague

SUNRISE SERENADE
Composer: Frankie Carle. Arranger: Bill Finegan. Recorded for Bluebird April 10, 1939

TRUMPETS	SAXOPHONES
Bob Price	Hal McIntyre
Mickey McMickle	Tex Beneke
Leigh Knowles	°Willie Schwartz
TROMBONES	Stanley Aronson
Glenn Miller	Al Klink
Al Mastren	PIANO
Paul Tanner	Chummy MacGregor
BASS	GUITAR
°Rolly Bundock	Allan Reuss
DRUMS	
Cody Sandifer	

REDSKIN RHUMBA
Composed and arranged by Charlie Barnet, based on Ray Noble's "Cherokee." Recorded for Bluebird October 14, 1940

TRUMPETS	SAXOPHONES
Bernie Privin	Charlie Barnet
°Billy May	Kurt Bloom
Sam Skolnick	Conn Humphreys
Lyman Vunk	Jimmy Lamare
TROMBONES	Leo White
Spud Murphy	PIANO
Don Ruppersberg	Bill Miller
Bill Robertson	GUITAR
Ford Leary	Bus Etri
DRUMS	BASS
Cliff Leeman	Phil Stephens

LONESOME ROAD
Nat Shilkret's copyrighted tune based on a traditional Negro work song. Arranger: Bill Finegan. Recorded for Victor May 1, 1939

TRUMPETS	SAXOPHONES
Andy Ferretti	Dean Kincaide
Peewee Erwin	Johnny Mince
Yank Lawson	°Babe Russin
TROMBONES	°Skeets Herfurt
Tommy Dorsey	Fred Stulce
Dave Jacobs	PIANO
Ward Silloway	Howard Smith
Elmer Smithers	GUITAR
BASS	Carmen Mastren
Gene Traxler	DRUMS
	Dave Tough

CIRIBIRIBIN
Composer: Alberto Pestalozza. Arrangers: Harry James and Jack Lawrence. Recorded for Columbia November 8-30, 1939

TRUMPETS	SAXOPHONES
Harry James	Dave Matthews
Jack Palmer	Drew Page
Claude Bowen	Claude Lakey
Jack Schaeffer	Bill Luther
TROMBONES	PIANO
Truett Jones	Jack Gardner
Dalton Rizzotto	GUITAR
Bruce Squires	Red Kent
DRUMS	BASS
Mickey Scrima	Thurman Teague

SWANEE RIVER
Composer: Stephen Foster. Arranger: Sy Oliver. Recorded for Victor October 16, 1940

TRUMPETS	SAXOPHONES
Ziggy Elman	Fred Stulce
Ray Linn	Johnny Mince
Chuck Peterson	Hymie Shertzer
TROMBONES	Heinie Beau
Tommy Dorsey	Don Lodice
Lowell Martin	PIANO
George Arus	Joe Bushkin
Les Jenkins	GUITAR
DRUMS	Clark Yocum
Buddy Rich	BASS
	Sid Weiss

MUSIC MAKERS
Composer: Harry James. Arranger: Jack Mathias. Recorded for Columbia January 8, 1941

TRUMPETS	SAXOPHONE
Harry James	Vido Musso
Claude Bowen	Claude Lakey
Al Stearns	°Chuck Gentry
Nick Buono	Johnny Mezey
TROMBONES	PIANO
Dalton Rizzotto	Al Lerner
°Hoyt Bohannon	GUITAR
Harry Rodgers	Ben Heller
DRUMS	BASS
Mickey Scrima	Thurman Teague

LET'S DANCE
Composers: Gregory Stone and Josef Bonime. Arranger: George Bassman. Recorded for Columbia October 24, 1939

TRUMPETS	CLARINET
Ziggy Elman	Benny Goodman
Jimmy Maxwell	SAXOPHONES
Johnny Martel	Toots Mondello
TROMBONES	Buff Estes
Vernon Brown	Bus Bassey
Red Ballard	Jerry Jerome
Ted Vesely	PIANO
BASS	Fletcher Henderson
Artie Bernstein	GUITAR
DRUMS	Charlie Christian
°Nick Fatool	

POMPTON TURNPIKE
Composer: Charlie Barnet. Arranger: °Billy May. Recorded for Bluebird July 19, 1940

TRUMPETS	SAXOPHONES
Bernie Privin	Charlie Barnet
°Billy May	Kurt Bloom
Sam Skolnick	Gene Kinsey
Lyman Vunk	Jimmy Lamare
TROMBONES	Leo White
Spud Murphy	PIANO
Don Ruppersberg	Bill Miller
Bill Robertson	GUITAR
DRUMS	Bus Etri
Cliff Leeman	BASS
	Phil Stephens

720 IN THE BOOKS
Composers: Jan Savitt and Johnny Watson. Arranger: Johnny Watson. Recorded for Decca September 21, 1939

TRUMPETS	SAXOPHONES
Jimmy Campbell	George Bohn
Johnny Austin	Jack Ferrier
Jack Hansen	Ed Clauson
TROMBONES	Frank Ludwig
Cutty Cutshall	PIANO
Don Sines	Gene DePaul
Al Leopold	GUITAR
DRUMS	Guy Smith
Russ Isaacs	BASS
	Morris Rayman

TAKE THE "A" TRAIN
Composer and arranger: Billy Strayhorn.
Recorded for Victor February 15, 1941

TRUMPETS
Wallace Jones
Ray Nance
Rex Stewart
TROMBONES
Juan Tizol
Lawrence Brown
Joe ("Tricky Sam")
Nanton
CLARINET
Barney Bigard
DRUMS
Sonny Greer

SAXOPHONES
Otto Hardwick
Johnny Hodges
Ben Webster
Harry Carney
PIANO
Duke Ellington
GUITAR
Fred Guy
BASS
Jimmy Blanton

SNOWFALL
Composer and arranger: Claude Thornhill.
Recorded for Columbia May 21, 1941

TRUMPETS
Conrad Gozzo

CLARINET
Irving Fazola

Rusty Dedrick
Bob Sprental
TROMBONES
Tasso Harris
Bob Jenney
BASS
Harvey Sell
DRUMS
Gene Leman

MOONLIGHT SERENADE
Composer and arranger: Glenn Miller.
Recorded for Bluebird April 4, 1939

TRUMPETS
Bob Price
Mickey McMickle
Leigh Knowles
TROMBONES
Glenn Miller
Al Mastren

SAXOPHONES
Hal McIntyre
Tex Beneke
° Willie Schwartz
Stanley Aronson
Al Klink

CLARINET &
SAXOPHONE
Dale Brown
Ted Goddard
George Paulsen
John Nelson
Hammond Russum
PIANO
Claude Thornhill
GUITAR
Alan Hanlon

Paul Tanner
BASS
° Rolly Bundock
DRUMS
Frank Carlson

ANVIL CHORUS
Composer: Giuseppe Verdi. Arranger: Jerry Gray. Recorded for Bluebird December 13-27, 1940

TRUMPETS
Mickey McMickle
Johnny Best
° Billy May
Ray Anthony
TROMBONES
Glenn Miller
Jim Priddy
Paul Tanner
Frank D'Annolfo
BASS
Trigger Alpert

PIANO
Chummy MacGregor
GUITAR
Allan Reuss

SAXOPHONES
Hal McIntyre
Tex Beneke
° Willie Schwartz
Ernie Caceres
Al Klink
PIANO
Chummy MacGregor
GUITAR
Jack Lathrop
DRUMS
Maurice Purtill

ACKNOWLEDGMENTS

Bradbury Thompson created the overall graphics design for "The Swing Era."

A number of musicians, band leaders, arrangers, singers, managers, song writers, and others knowledgeable on swing music helped with source material for this book. The editors wish to thank particularly the following for their assistance: Willard Alexander, Trigger Alpert, Charlie Barnet, Bill Borden, Les Brown, Pete Candoli, Julian Dash, Bruce Davidson, George Dixon, Bob Eberly, Bill Finegan, Chuck Gentry, Joe Graves, Jerry Gray, Bobby Hackett, John Hammond, Skeets Herfurt, Earl Hines, Louise Tobin Hucko, Peanuts Hucko, Harry James, Amy Lee, Gene Krupa, Lew McCreary, Ray McKinley, Chummy MacGregor, Jack Marshall, Billy May, Johnny Mercer, Alan P. Merriam, Frank Monte, Abe Most, Sy Oliver, Bernie Privin, Andy Razaf, Eddie Sauter, Artie Shaw, Shorty Sherock, Charlie Spivak, Larry Wagner and Helen Ward.

Many Time Inc. departments and staff members were involved in the initial preparation for this series. A few of them are: Anne Drayton and Carmela Lotrecchiano of the office of LIFE's Director of Photography; Marcia Gauger, Nancy Faber and Barbara Wilkins of the Time-Life News Service; Doris O'Neil, Chief, Time Inc. Picture Collection; George Karas and Herbert Orth of the Photographic Laboratory.

Special thanks go to Stanley Gruber and Larry Parker for help in locating rare recordings.

CREDITS

Slipcases & Cover—Gjon Mili
4—Bernard Hoffman
6—l. Acme; t.c. courtesy Joan S. Reiter; t.r. United Press Photo; b. Hutchinson & Co. Ltd.
7—l. International News Photo; c.t. Whittier College Yearbook; r. Andre De Dienes
9—l. Nina Leen; t.r. George Karger, Pix;
11—Alfred Eisenstaedt
12, 13—Jack Birns, Graphic House, Inc.
14—Carl M. Mydans
15—Associated Press
16—Alfred Eisenstaedt

17—Nina Leen
18, 19—Elmer Staab, Milwaukee Journal
20—t.l. Ralph Crane; t.r. Walter Sanders, Black Star; b. Nina Leen
22—Hansel Meith exc. b. Hart Preston
24—l. & c. Peter Stackpole; r.t. & b. Alfred Eisenstaedt
25—Peter Stackpole
26, 27—t.l. Walter Sanders, Black Star; t.r. George Karger, Pix; b. Myron Davis
28, 29—t.l. John Phillips; t.r. Margaret Bourke-White; b. Eliot Elisofon
30—t. Miami Herald; b. Gordon Coster

31—George Karger, Pix
32—Peter Stackpole
33—Courtesy Mr. & Mrs. Frank M. Titelman. Photograph, Sabine Weiss
35—Carl Iwasaki
36, 37—Photo Files
38—t. Photo Files; b. Culver Pictures
39—t. Photo Files; b. N. Nelson Morris, Black Star
40—Down Beat
41—Johnny Florea
42—t. Culver Pictures; c. Museum of Modern Art/Film Stills Archive; b. Lisa Larsen

43—t. Frank Ippolito; b. Charles E. Steinheimer
45—Frank Ippolito
46—Down Beat
48, 49—Photo Files
50—Culver Pictures
51—George Karger, Pix
52, 53—l.t. & b. Frank Monte; t.c. Photo Files; t. rt. Peter Stackpole; b. Museum of Modern Art/Film Stills Archive
55—Frank Monte

Abbreviations: b., bottom; c., center; exc., except; l., left; r., right; t., top

64

XXX